ECONOMICS
50 KEY IDEAS UNPACKED

ECONOMICS
50 KEY IDEAS UNPACKED

TEJVAN PETTINGER

This edition published in 2025 by Arcturus Publishing Limited
26/27 Bickels Yard, 151–153 Bermondsey Street,
London SE1 3HA

AD011901UK

Printed in the UK

Contents

Introduction

The impact of economics is all around us, and yet understanding how these economic forces affect our lives can be hard.

This book aims to help explain these concepts so that we can make more sense of the big economic issues which affect us. One of the challenges in studying economics is knowing where to start; some issues have so many variables and complexities that they can be difficult to grasp. In this book we will explain the essential concepts first, and use these as building blocks to gain a better understanding of this fascinating subject.

One way of approaching economics is to consider two different branches of economics – micro- and macroeconomics. Microeconomics is all the relatively small issues, such as individual markets, how firms operate, and the workings of the economy. For example, have you ever wondered about whether we benefit from new technology? In the eighteenth century some workers were so enraged when more productive machines replaced their skilled work, they took to smashing them up. These workers were later given the rather pejorative label of 'Luddites' and the Luddite fallacy is the concept that it is a mistake to view new technology as harmful to our overall economic prospects.

While we can sympathize with skilled workers left without a good paying job, I think very few of us would wish to turn back the clock to the living standards of the 18th century. For all the problems in modern economies, it is worth noting the very significant improvements in living standards which have occurred in the past few centuries. Economics has been fundamental to enable rapid change – in both living standards and social opportunities.

This is the realm of macroeconomics – looking at the whole economic picture and how national economies have fared in a global economy.

If we lose our job, that is a microeconomic issue. By contrast, a rise in mass unemployment becomes a national problem and an economic issue where the government may need to intervene.

It is this macroeconomic picture which will appear most regularly on the daily news. Why does inflation suddenly surge? Should we

We can divide economics into two branches: microeconomics and macroeconomics.

worry about a trade deficit with China? Understanding these subjects can enable us to have a better comprehension of why prices are rising or living standards stagnating.

Of course, the distinction between macro- and microeconomics is somewhat artificial. A rise in oil prices affects both local market segments, with higher petrol prices, but also the whole global economy, bringing the threat of inflation and lower growth.

I hope that by reading this book, you will learn that economics is as much an art as a science. Mathematics can give us correct, definitive answers, but economics is complex, and we need to be sensitive to different possibilities and different solutions. Economics cannot be reduced to a simple ideology or a simplistic response. They say, ask seven economists a question and you might get eight different answers. Frustrating maybe, but it does make things interesting! Even in the case of the Luddite fallacy, you will see later that there are still reasons to be wary of a rapid deployment of new technology.

If you are interested in gaining a wider understanding and perspective on the economy we live in, this book will help to shine a light on these topics.

1
Money

Money is widely accepted as a means of exchange. Money also has other functions: a store of wealth, a form of deferred payment (debts) and a unit of account to give a relative measure of value.

Most forms of money are issued by a country's central bank, which acts as a guarantor for the money that it issues. Without money, economies would need to rely on a barter-style system where individuals swap goods and services. Money is a key factor that enables us to specialize in certain jobs, so we can get paid in money without needing to produce specific goods to barter.

INTRINSIC MONEY

Money developed from being tied to a material with an intrinsic value. For example, it was easy to develop gold coins, because there was a strong value to the gold itself. Even if you cut a gold coin in half, there was still an intrinsic value for those pieces of gold. The problem with relying solely on precious metals is that it limits the amount of money that can be in circulation. Also, the price of gold can fluctuate due to speculation, meaning that the value of gold coins may not be as constant as we think.

What is money? In the early days it was gold coins, but in modern times it includes paper money and electronic balances at your bank.

FIAT MONEY

Early banks began to issue paper notes, which promised to pay the bearer a sum of gold on production of this paper note. As long as individuals trusted the financial institution issuing the paper note, this 'fiat money' – money with no intrinsic value – can be used and recognized as legal tender. In modern times, most money exists as electronic deposits in commercial banks. We trust that if we go to the bank to withdraw cash, the bank will be able to give the cash we demand to withdraw. To ensure the stability of the banking system, a central bank acts as lender of last resort. So if a commercial bank runs short of money, it can go to the main central bank and request the shortfall in cash. If necessary, a central bank can print (or create) money to meet any liquidity shortages.

MONEY SUPPLY

What is the amount of money in circulation at the moment? At the start of 2021, there was US $2.04 trillion in circulation, though an estimated 50% of this currency is circulating outside the United States. However, this cash is only part of the nation's money supply. A wider definition is known as M0 or the monetary base. This includes cash but also commercial banks' operational deposits at the Federal Reserve. The monetary base has increased significantly since 2008 due to the process of quantitative easing. However, even this monetary base is only a small part of the effective money in the economy. A wider definition of money includes not just cash but also saving deposits in banks and deposits in retail money markets. In 2021, the broader M2 measure of money supply in the United States stands at $21 trillion. M2 is a measure of the money supply that includes cash, deposits, and assets that can be easily converted into cash.

NEAR MONEY

There are some financial objects that can be classified as near money. This means that they do have a store of value, but it is not seamless to convert into a medium of exchange. For example, with a debit card you can use your electronic bank reserves to buy goods, but a government bond would not be accepted as payment. However, you could easily sell on a bond market and gain the cash to buy the good. Therefore, it is close to money, but not meeting sufficient criteria to be classified as money.

M2 money supply in the United States

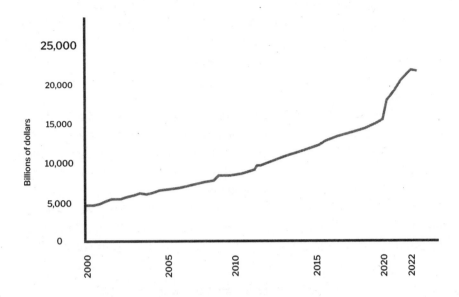

There was a surge in the US money supply in 2021 due to the monetary and fiscal stimulus to deal with Covid.

BITCOIN AND CRYPTOCURRENCY

In recent years, new forms of money such as bitcoin have been created. The idea was to create a form of money that did not rely on monetary authorities and there was no possibility of inflation because there is only a fixed amount of bitcoin in existence. In theory, bitcoin meets some of the functions of money because some people accept it as a means of exchange, and it can be used to value a limited range of goods and services (often on the black market). However, its lack of universal acceptance means bitcoin cannot be equated with money. If you tried to pay your gas bill or student loan with bitcoin, it would not be accepted. Some places will

Cryptocurrencies like Bitcoin are a new form of money that have emerged in the 21st century.

convert bitcoin to cash, but this is not a seamless transaction. Also, the value of bitcoin and new cryptocurrencies has proved to be very volatile, the prices fluctuating due to market sentiment, highlighting its transitory nature. Thus, when trying to sell bitcoin for cash, many investors found the value was much less than they hoped.

PRINTING MONEY

One issue with central banks controlling the supply of money is that there is a temptation for governments to deal with economic crises by printing money. Printing money is a temporary solution that enables the government to pay for goods or pay workers, but it does not create output or deal with the underlying economic problem. When the supply of money doubles but the amount of goods stays the same, the economy will see more money chasing the same amount of goods. Firms will respond to the higher monetary demand by putting up prices. In other

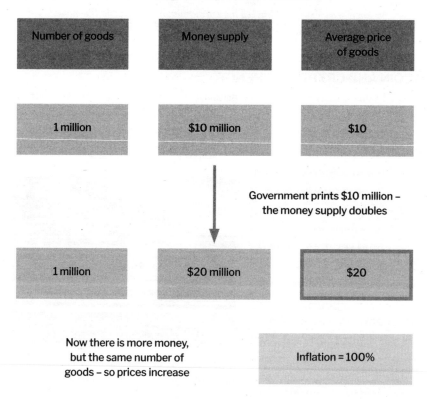

Printing money causes inflation

Number of goods	Money supply	Average price of goods
1 million	$10 million	$10
1 million	$20 million	$20

Government prints $10 million – the money supply doubles

Now there is more money, but the same number of goods – so prices increase

Inflation = 100%

words, printing money is usually inflationary, and workers enjoy only the illusion of higher incomes. In the past, quite a few economies have got into serious difficulties through increasing the money supply faster than real output. For a country in economic crisis, printing money can only be a very temporary solution, and can soon make it worse by causing hyperinflation (see page 84).

This is not to say that printing money always causes inflation. In some circumstances, such as a deep recession, printing more money may not be inflationary because commercials banks are still reluctant to lend and firms reluctant to invest. In a period of deflation (falling prices – see pages 85–88), printing money may cause only very moderate inflation and not be a problem.

2
Economic Growth

Economic growth is an increase in the value and size of a country's economy. It means an increase in national income and national output.

All things being equal, economic growth should lead to people being economically better off, with a higher standard of living. Economic growth has many benefits, especially for developing economies with widespread poverty and low living standards. Economic growth has been a key factor in reducing absolute poverty in the world during the past 40 years.

In the 20th century (and still today), economic growth has often been held up as the holy grail of economic policy – increase output, increase incomes. But, environmental concerns have increasingly led people to question the value of economic growth, with some arguing the benefits are now outweighing the costs.

BENEFITS OF GROWTH
World economic growth since 1820

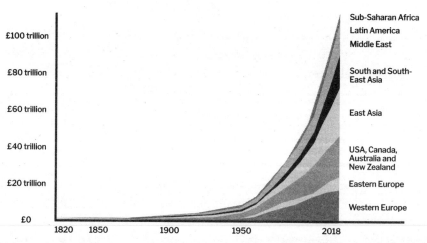

Economic growth has played a major role in reducing poverty.

Before we consider the problems of economic growth, it is worth bearing in mind that very few of us would prefer to go back to the living standards of the 19th century, when life expectancy was 50% lower, poverty was widespread, housing was of poor quality and many workers were malnourished. Economic growth has enabled the majority of the population to escape from absolute poverty and live where the basic necessities of life are met. This is no small achievement. Even in the past 30 years, 20% of the world's population have been lifted out of absolute poverty due to economic growth. It is one of the success stories of modern life (though often overlooked). While we tend to focus on the problems of the world, even a modest amount of economic growth can transform life for many.

Economic growth has additional benefits. With increasing output, firms will be willing to take on more workers, helping to reduce unemployment. With higher national output, governments will be able to collect more tax revenue (even if tax rates stay the same). This higher tax revenue can be used to fund healthcare, education, transport and policies to protect the environment. In 1950, shortly after World War II, the UK government's national debt to GDP ratio reached over 220%. This sounds very intimidating. But

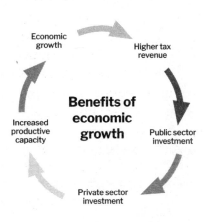

five decades of fairly constant economic growth reduced the debt to GDP ratio to 40% by 2000. This is one reason why governments love economic growth – it helps improve a nation's finances, enabling them to pursue voter-friendly policies such as lower tax and/or higher spending.

COSTS OF ECONOMIC GROWTH

The problem with economic growth occurs when we seek it at all costs, ignoring other objectives. The first major issue is how economic growth can conflict with the environment. For example, economic growth will lead to greater consumption of natural resources, more burning of fossil fuels, increased air pollution and the loss of habitats such as forests to enable more cattle farming. The consequence of this is a rise in external costs to the rest of the world. The external costs of pollution include

Economic growth can lead to higher living standards, lower unemployment and higher government tax revenues.

Deforestation in the Amazon rainforest in Brazil.

health costs, lower life expectancy and the possibility that it will be impossible to live in some regions of the world in the future. Therefore, if we look only at the raw data of gross domestic product (GDP) – in other words, only at how much is produced – we ignore all the negative impacts of growth on actual living standards.

A key issue is how economic growth is achieved. If an economy were to dramatically increase the burning of fossil fuels, working longer hours and building up its military, this increased output would be reflected in higher GDP. However, these three examples may all cause a fall in living standards – more pollution and less leisure time, while weapons are, by definition, designed to destroy. However, equally, we could have economic growth caused in a very different way. Suppose we install efficient solar panels to generate more power than old coal plants: we see an increase in GDP, but at the same time a rise in living standards due to cheaper, cleaner electricity.

Similarly, effective new technology will enable higher labour productivity. With greater automation and artificial intelligence, we can produce the same number of goods with fewer workers. This would (in theory) then enable higher pay, and more leisure time.

Economic growth from a low level of economic development is likely to have a large rise in living standards, but as we get richer, economic growth increasingly has diminishing returns. For many, an increase in income of just £1,000 a year makes a big difference. But a millionaire who has the same increase – from £1,000,000 to £1,001,000 – will hardly notice.

Economic growth gives an imperfect guide to living standards. But if we want to evaluate living standards, it is better to focus on specific measures of living standards, such as Measures of Economic Welfare (MEW) and the Human Happiness Index (HHI). These generally use economic growth as a starting point, but also include other measurable factors, such as life expectancy, quantity of education and the environment.

CAUSES OF ECONOMIC GROWTH

There are two main causes of economic growth – increase in demand (more spending and investment) and an increase in production (higher output). In the long term, the key factor for determining economic growth is the rate at which productive capacity rises. In turn, this depends on the amount of resources (land, labour, capital) and the productivity of these resources. For example, the development of electricity enabled a significant rise in labour productivity because it is much more efficient to use a power tool than do everything manually. When individual workers can produce more goods, the whole economy will be able to produce more.

Causes of economic growth

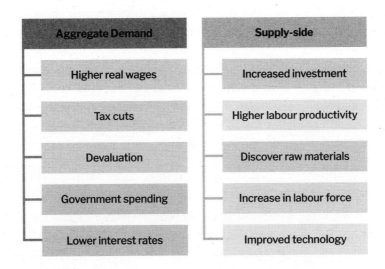

Also, when workers are more productive, a firm will gain more revenue from selling more or better goods. Therefore, the firm can afford to pay higher wages to workers. As workers see a rise in pay, this will increase demand for goods in the economy. A good example is the introduction of the assembly line around the turn of the century. Initially cars were made by hand and were very expensive, the preserve of the rich. But Henry Ford produced cars on a mass scale, using division of labour and an assembly line, which dramatically increased efficiency. Ford could now sell cars at a fraction of the price, causing a surge in demand for cars. Also, Ford was able to significantly increase wages for workers. In effect, a car worker could now afford to buy a car he helped produce – something unthinkable a decade previously. In a nutshell, this is the essence of economic growth – rising productivity, enabling more output and rising wages, enabling more demand.

3
Limits to Economic Growth

We have become used to the ideal of increasing economic growth, and politicians often prioritize it above all other objectives.

However, we are increasingly aware of the potential limitations. As far back as 1798 Thomas Malthus wrote 'An Essay on the Principle of Population', in which he warned that increasing the food supply would only encourage a higher population that, in turn, would be unable to feed itself. For this reason, he was pessimistic about the chances of increasing per capita income. Fortunately, the gloomy prognosis of Malthus was proved to be inaccurate. Food production has been increased – not by using more land but thanks to higher productivity and better technology. The limits to growth that Malthus foresaw did not occur. Improved productivity and farming techniques have increased both the population and per capita incomes.

ENVIRONMENTAL CONCERNS

However, although it is easy to dismiss Malthus, there are in the 21st century increasingly clear limits to economic growth. Firstly, there is concern about access to basic resources that we have taken for granted – water and useable farmland. A combination of global warming, poor management and a growing population has led to the increased desertification of large areas of sub-Saharan Africa and other places around the world. This will place

Thomas Malthus.

Kuznets curve

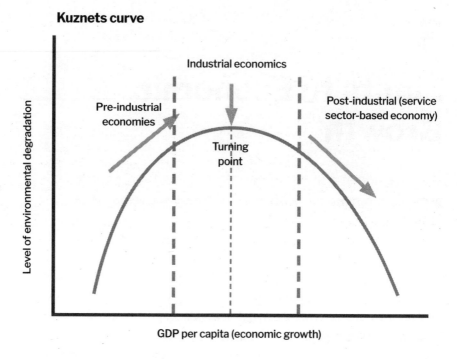

Higher growth initially causes environmental costs, but the right technology can lead to less environmental damage.

limits on future economic growth and even the viability of particular communities. The UN warn that access to clean drinking water may be the great concern for future generations around the world. If climate change does disrupt usual farming activity, the foundations of our economies could be undermined, leading to a loss of global output.

Malthus was proved wrong because in the nineteenth century there were easy productivity gains from better technology. However, technological innovation is subject to diminishing returns. A small amount of fertilizer can increase output significantly, but using more leads to diminishing returns. Also, technology can prove to have unintended consequences in the long term. For example, the use of pesticides can increase crop yields in the short term. However, they have also been blamed for a long-term decline in insect populations. And if we reach a tipping point in the number of bees or pollinating insects, this could threaten the survival of food production because crops cannot be sufficiently pollinated.

GROWTH AND A BETTER ENVIRONMENT

Some economists are more optimistic about economic growth and the environment. The environmental Kuznets curve acknowledges that economic growth does initially lead to an increase in pollution and damage to the environment. However, when an economy reaches a certain income level, the economy is able to devote more resources to improving the environment and prioritizing long-term sustainability. For example, in the early years of industrialization, economies burnt coal which caused severe air pollution. But in the post-war period, those same economies legislated to limit pollution emissions and mandate a shift to less polluting energy sources. Therefore, it is possible to have economic growth with declining pollution levels. For example, in the UK, CO_2 emissions peaked in the mid-1960s and by 2022 had fallen to levels not seen since the nineteenth century.

Also, an optimistic view of the limits of economic growth argues that if commodities do start to become scarce, then the market mechanism will force prices to rise and provide the incentive to reduce demand and find viable alternatives.

COSTS OF ECONOMIC GROWTH

However, this rose-tinted view of economic growth and environmental sustainability is misleading. It is true that some visible pollutants can fall as the economy develops. For example, new technology made it relatively painless to ban coal-powered heating in city centres. However, while some visible pollutants have fallen, there is an ever-growing increase in less visible toxins and external pollutants – some of which we may not be fully aware of until later. For example, pollution levels of nitrogen dioxide are still high in city centres. More seriously, even if one country does reduce CO_2 emissions, what counts is the global level, with rising global CO_2 emissions linked to global warming and potentially devastating impacts on the long-term sustainability of normal economic activity. Also, a problem is that the market mechanism can fail when the costs of economic growth are only really noticed by future generations. With pollution from coal-powered stations, we may wish to act to reduce the smog over cities. But with global warming, when the earth reaches a tipping point, it may be too late to reverse past trends to ensure the sustainability of the environment for normal economic growth.

OTHER LIMITS TO GROWTH

Apart from the environment and sustainability of natural resources, are there any other limits to economic growth? In recent years, the rate of economic growth in major advanced countries has slowed down. This is especially true in countries such as Japan, which has an ageing population and a decline in the working age population. One reason put forward for slowing growth rates is diminishing returns from scientific and technological advances. In the past, some technologies enabled a step change in productivity – steam power, electricity, assembly lines, microchips. However, to get the same quantum leap in technological progress is becoming harder. Despite artificial intelligence and increased use of robots, productivity growth has slowed down. Combined with demographic changes, this is leading to lower levels of investment and research. It is worth bearing in mind, though, that in the past people have often assumed we have reached peak productivity, only to be proved wrong, and there is great scope for radical new energy sources that could provide cheap, renewable energies.

A final thought is that one limit to growth may be that in the future the desirability of economic growth is reduced as people prefer to reprioritize from maximizing GDP to maximizing quality of life. This may lead to more leisure time and lower consumption.

4
Supply and Demand

Supply and demand is a fundamental aspect of economics which permeates our daily life, whether we are aware of it or not. The forces of supply and demand determine prices, influence the goods we buy, and set the wages we receive.

Demand refers to the amount of goods we are willing to buy at different prices. Usually as price rises, demand will fall. This is for two reasons. As prices rise, we can afford less because our effective income falls. Rising prices of gas encourage us to use less – we don't have any alternative to gas central heating, but higher gas prices reduce our disposable income, forcing us to use less. Another reason is that as prices rise, we will look for alternatives. If the price of Nestle coffee increases by 20%, this will encourage us to switch to an alternative brand, such as Kenco.

Supply is the amount of goods that firms are willing to sell on the market at different prices. The supply curve is upward sloping because higher prices make it more profitable for firms to supply.

The real magic comes when we bring supply and demand together. There is a sweet spot (or equilibrium point) where supply and demand meet, creating an equilibrium in the market. Let's use as an example takeaway coffee. If the market price was £1, few firms would be willing to supply coffee at that price, but the demand would be high. Why bother making coffee at home, when it is nearly as cheap to buy on the move? But this price would lead to a shortage: the demand would be much greater

The price of coffee beans is determined by supply and demand.

Supply and demand

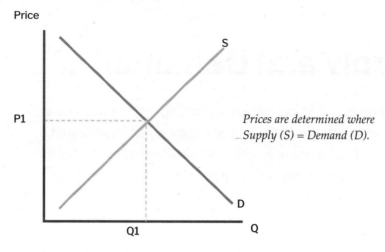

Price

S

P1

Prices are determined where Supply (S) = Demand (D).

D

Q1   Q

than supply, and you would find long queues as customers sought to purchase coffee from the limited suppliers. However, if the price rose to £3.10, say, this is the point where supply meets demand and there is no tendency for the price to change in the short term.

The remarkable thing is that in most market-based economies, there is no authority or plan to set prices. The prices are simply determined by the market – or, as Adam Smith put it, 'the invisible hand of the market'. If coffee became more fashionable, we would likely see a rise in market demand, and this would lead to higher prices.

The invisible hand is so called because nobody consciously sets out to set the market price; individuals just pursue their own self-interest. Firms will respond to their profit motive and if prices are high, sell more. Consumers on their part will buy the goods only if they get value (utility) from the purchase. Adam Smith, the 'father of economics', explained it thus:

> *Every individual… neither intends to promote the public interest, nor knows how much he is promoting it… he intends only his own security; and by directing that industry in such a manner as its produce may be of the greatest value, he intends only his own gain, and he is in this, as in many other cases, led by an invisible hand to promote an end which was no part of his intention.*

The Wealth Of Nations (1776)

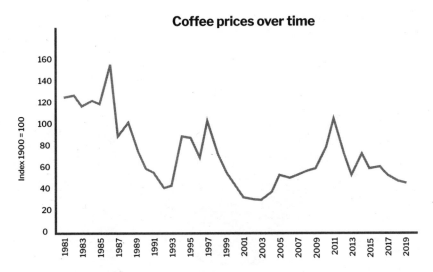

Coffee prices over time

The price of coffee is quite volatile because supply can be affected by the weather.

The price of takeaway coffee is fairly stable (subject just to steady inflationary increases). However, if we look at the supply and demand for a coffee bean, the raw commodity price is much more volatile. This is because the supply and demand can fluctuate due to factors such as weather, diseases, crop failure and efforts to form a cartel (restrict supply to maximize price for farmers).

The graph above shows that between 1986 and 1992 the price of coffee fell 72%. The reason for the prolonged fall in price was a growth in supply of coffee beans as more countries across the world expanded production and the amount of coffee beans sold on the world market rose. As supply was growing much faster than demand, prices fell. However, within two years, 1992–1994, the price of coffee doubled as the supply of coffee fell due to bad weather and efforts to restrict the supply of coffee.

A key component of supply and demand is the idea that firms and individuals have the ability to decide how to use their economic resources. In a planned economy, like the Soviet Union, supply and demand were not used to determine prices. Quantity and prices were set by a central authority, which told factories how much they needed to produce and what price to charge. The advantage of this is that basic commodities like bread could be kept cheap.

But the big problem is that a central planning authority has poor information about what products will be needed and there is great inflexibility if market conditions change. This can easily lead to the

A shortage at a Moscow supermarket, 1990.

shortages and surpluses that we saw in communist economies. In a free market, market forces / the invisible hand enable firms and individuals to decide what to produce, how to produce it and for whom. The market is constantly evolving as consumer behaviour and supplies change. The goods in short supply will increase in price as the market reflects their relative scarcity. Goods which are oversupplied will see a fall in price.

Supply and demand is very useful: without it the economy would be much more inefficient, and we would find it harder to get many goods. However, market forces and the invisible hand can lead to unwelcome outcomes. For example, many young people find the cost of renting a place to live is very expensive, and buying a house is out of reach. This is the unfortunate outcome of market forces; a limited supply but growing demand pushes prices up and makes the cost of living very onerous. In 2022, gas and electricity prices shot up due to restrictions in supply. This has reduced the quality of life for many on low incomes – an unfortunate example of supply and demand in action.

5
Opportunity Cost

Opportunity cost is the next best alternative foregone. It is what we miss out on when we choose one option over another. Every decision in life has some kind of opportunity cost, whether we are conscious of it or not.

Sometimes opportunity cost may seem quite straightforward. If we go out with friends, the opportunity cost is that we cannot stay in and work. If we spend our last £100 on food, we can't spend that money on entertainment. However, opportunity costs can be less visible than the actual monetary costs we face.

Suppose we are buying a new house and we are weighing up the choice between one costing £190,000 and £200,000. We will weigh up which house is better value for money and whether we can afford the more expensive one. Another consideration is that if we buy the more expensive house, the opportunity cost is that we will not have that extra £10,000 to spend on home improvements.

Suppose we buy a new car for £15,000 and a few years later, its value falls to £3,000. What is the opportunity cost of keeping the car and not selling? Here the initial cost is not relevant. The opportunity cost is only the £3,000 we could get from selling. The initial price does not impact on our present opportunity cost.

If you buy one house, the opportunity cost is the different house you can no longer buy.

The opportunity cost of doing the cleaning yourself is that you lose time.

Suppose you spend £5 every day on drinking two beers. In one sense, that seems quite a low price for a small daily pleasure. But what is the opportunity cost involved? From a simple perspective, it could be £5 that you don't spend on better quality food or a new book. But, suppose instead of spending £5 each day, you invested that spare cash in a savings account, which gives an annual interest of 3%. After three years of daily saving, you would have £5,657.19. When we spend on small daily purchases, we rarely think in terms of this kind of opportunity cost. But, three years of drinking no beer may mean we have nearly £6,000 to spend on buying a new car. Equally, you could turn this equation on its head and say that the opportunity cost of being austere and always saving for the future is that you miss out on life's little luxuries. Maybe if you stop drinking you spend less time socializing with friends. You could have £6,000 in three years' time and feel like you missed out. The opportunity cost will depend on individual circumstances and what you think is important. For someone else, no beers for three years may not only save them money but help them lose weight and improve their health. In this case, the daily beer drinking not only has a high financial cost, but also the less visible opportunity costs, such as the effect on your health.

SHOULD WE PAY FOR A CLEANER?

Suppose you earn £10 an hour. There is no point in paying a cleaner £20 an hour to clean your house. The opportunity cost of spending one hour cleaning is only the £10 you could have made working in your job, which is less than the price of hiring a cleaner. But, if you are a business executive earning £200 an hour, the opportunity cost of spending an hour cleaning is equivalent to losing £200 from doing your job. Therefore, a business executive may feel the very high opportunity cost of doing manual labour means it makes sense to employ someone else. For a low-paid worker, it will not.

GOVERNMENT OPPORTUNITY COST

When it comes to elections, politicians (and voters) are never so keen to stipulate all the opportunity costs of decisions. If the government promises tax cuts, the immediate effect of lower tax rates is clear. The opportunity costs, though, are less visible, and will take the form of reduced government spending (on health or education, say) and / or higher government borrowing. The wish list of voters usually involves both lower taxes and higher spending (on schemes that concern them). The difficulty is that this ignores the opportunity cost of both lower taxes and higher spending. During the COVID pandemic, governments were faced with difficult choices in opportunity cost: the trade-off between protecting health and the impact on people's freedoms and economic activity.

To limit the spread of infectious diseases at any time, the government can mandate workers to stay at home. The benefits are lower transmission, less hospital admissions and fewer deaths. However, the opportunity cost is the loss of freedom to individuals and the financial hit to certain sectors of the economy – especially hospitality, which was impacted by lockdown mandates. As usual, the opportunity cost scenarios work both ways. If a government opens up an economy when a disease is still spreading rapidly, there will be a cost to hospitals which are faced with a rise in transmissions. There will even be an opportunity cost to those who are not themselves infected but who cannot get treatment for other diseases affecting them, like cancer.

COVID forced big choices. The opportunity cost of free movement was a rise in cases. The opportunity cost of reducing the virus was loss of freedom.

6
Division of Labour

Division of labour refers to how workers specialize in different jobs. We don't try to be a jack of all trades but concentrate on one particular task within the economy.

It is division of labour which has been a key driving force of productivity growth and higher living standards. One thousand years ago, the majority of people worked as farmers, growing their own food and preparing it. There was a limited division of labour, but in a modern economy there is very significant division of labour. For example, one farmer can grow enough food for thousands of people, enabling other workers to concentrate on tasks such as designing packaging, transporting the good and research into the best food preparation.

The advantage of division of labour is that workers can become highly skilled in one particular area of work – without requiring excessive amounts of training. A modern good like a computer is full of intricate components. If you asked a person to make a computer from scratch, it would be impossible. However, if a group of workers focus on designing and building chips and another concentrates on programming, this separation of tasks makes the project possible. As products become more sophisticated, there is an ever-growing division of labour. You might ask where an iPhone is built. The answer is, all over the place. It is designed in California; the touchscreen technology is built in the United States, Israel and Greece; and the phone itself is assembled in China, Thailand and Malaysia. Every component of the iPhone, from battery to LCD screen and touch ID, represents a division of

An iPhone is a very complex product, which requires thousands of different types of workers.

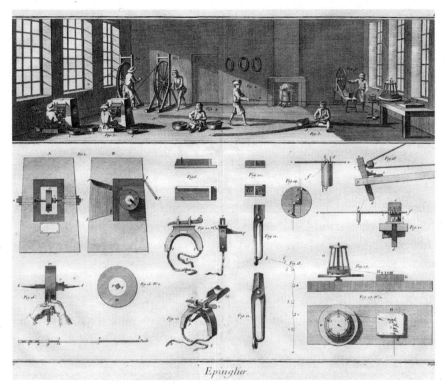

A pin factory in Adam Smith's time (from Denis Diderot's Encyclopédie *of 1751–66).*

labour: there are firms specializing in one area, and within a firm, workers are divided into different aspects of production.

In fact, the manufacture of an iPhone is so complex, it can be hard to visualize the amount of specialist components and workers that go into making the final product. In his book *An Inquiry into the Nature and Causes of the Wealth of Nations* (1776), Adam Smith investigated a pin factory, and found that when workers were divided into different areas of work, efficiency was vastly increased. The difference was that if a worker had to make a pin, he had to move around and do many different jobs. But when there was some kind of assembly line and the pin came to workers, they were able to do one very simple job such as stretching the metal, cutting the metal and shaping the pin head. The pin factory was a very early example of mass production. This is something Henry Ford would popularize when he introduced the assembly line for making Model-T cars. Ford wasn't the first to introduce an assembly line, but he was able to produce spectacular benefits, all through the division of labour and giving workers very limited but particular tasks.

DRAWBACK OF DIVISION OF LABOUR

When you were a self-sufficient farmer, you may not have been very efficient, but you could get a strong sense of self-worth from growing and producing your own food. You felt a strong connection with your job because you could see what you were making and how it helps you. Fast-forward 100 years, and the same workers may be earning 100 times more working on a modern assembly line, but the work is very boring, tedious and there is little sense of accomplishment if all you do every day is to bash a strip of metal to make a pin. Ford found that even very high wages were not enough to prevent a high turnover of workers. For some, division of labour enables very attractive and worthwhile jobs – for designers, writers, and those engaged in a creative process – but for others, division of labour can mean very tedious and unrewarding jobs doing manual labour.

ECONOMIES OF SCALE

A by-product of division of labour is that it creates economies of scale. This means that as output increases, average costs fall. If you need to produce only one car, there is no point in having a large assembly line and division of labour. A highly specialized factory with 1,000 workers

The Ford assembly line in 1913.

making up an assembly line is worthwhile only if you are making a very substantial number of cars. More division of labour within economies accelerated the trend to mass production and mass consumption. The more that was produced, the more labour could specialize. The more that labour has specialized, the more efficient production has become.

FUTURE DIVISION OF LABOUR

With ever-growing technology, labour is increasingly specialized into highly skilled jobs like programming and IT development. Some workers still do highly repetitive tasks such as packing boxes in a warehouse, but even this is becoming automated, with robots and drones able to do jobs currently done by humans. This will leave workers to move to jobs that cannot be fully replicated by robots – such as physiotherapy or nursing.

7
Marginal Revolution

Every economy works, or fails, by a process of supplying the goods, services and resources for which there is a demand. Supply and demand are therefore the main forces acting in an economy.

The margin is an important concept in economics. It refers to the last unit consumed, produced or sold and can refer to the extra utility or additional revenue gained. For example, the marginal cost of producing one extra item is the addition to total cost from producing one extra unit. If a restaurant produces 10 meals at a total cost of £150, the average cost is £15. But, suppose producing an 11th meal increased the total cost to £157, then the marginal cost of that 11th meal is just £7 – very different to the average cost of producing a meal.

IMPORTANCE OF MARGINAL COST

To build an offshore wind farm will incur millions of pounds in the fixed cost of building the wind turbines. A firm may have to spend £1 billion even before it starts producing any electricity. But once the turbines

The marginal cost of producing wind energy is very low.

have been built, the marginal cost of producing electricity is relatively low. They will keep producing electricity without any expensive inputs. There will be some maintenance costs, but the main ingredient – wind – is free. If we compare this to a coal power station, there will be high fixed costs in building too, but the firm will also need to keep buying coal, so the marginal cost of producing coal-powered electricity is likely to be higher than the marginal cost of producing electricity from renewable sources. This difference in marginal cost matters for energy policy because once the investment in the infrastructure of renewable energy has been made, the marginal cost of producing electricity is lower.

USING MARGINAL COST TO SET PRICES

When firms look at pricing decisions, it becomes very important to consider the marginal cost – and not just the average costs. For example, suppose the Eurostar train company has unsold seats on a train journey, what price should it charge? In this case, the important consideration is not the total cost of the train journey but the marginal cost of an extra passenger. If a train is passing from London to Paris, the cost is mostly the same, whether it is empty or full. If the train is 50% full, selling extra tickets will have only a very low marginal cost – possibly the extra weight of passengers may require more fuel, and more time for passengers to board the train. Those extra passengers are a very low marginal cost and therefore, even if Eurostar sells last-minute tickets at a low price, the company can increase its total profit.

However, if we took a very different industry like tap water, how does marginal cost differ? In this case, producing higher quantities of

When a train is travelling, the marginal cost of extra passengers is quite low.

William Stanley Jevons, one of the founders of marginal utility theory.

tap water can have higher marginal costs. Suppose a town needs only a small quantity of water. It can collect rainwater for free – low marginal cost. If more is required, it can use a local river. But, if demand keeps rising, the town may need to build expensive reservoirs in areas with high rainfall and then pipe that water. Therefore, it is a mistake to think that consuming more tap water has very low marginal cost – as society produces more, it can require more expensive infrastructure. This is why water companies would like to introduce water meters, so we pay for extra units of water consumed and not have unlimited water consumption.

MARGINAL UTILITY

In the mid to late nineteenth century, economists such as William Jevons, Léon Walras and Carl Menger all developed theories to explain consumer behaviour. They observed that when deciding what to consume, individuals try to evaluate how much satisfaction they will get from that extra unit. They term this the marginal utility from consuming more of a good.

TOO MUCH OF A GOOD THING

For example, if we really like chocolate, why don't we eat it all the time? The answer is that the marginal utility (the marginal satisfaction of chocolate) is changing. Our first chocolate bar of the week gives a high level of satisfaction. We feel like we are treating ourselves and we enjoy the taste. However, if we were to have another chocolate bar straight after the first, the marginal utility – the satisfaction we gain – would fall quite significantly. After eating the second chocolate bar, we are already feeling quite full, perhaps even a little guilty. Therefore, when deciding what and how much to buy, we are constantly considering the marginal benefit of a good. 'You can have too much of a good thing' is an old

A diamond and water have very different uses and costs of production.

saying that is really highlighting the fact that the marginal utility of our favourite goods can quickly fall. We really like chocolate, but we don't want to eat it all the time because it will make us feel sick and soon have negative satisfaction.

THE PARADOX OF VALUE

A good example of the importance of marginal analysis in economics is given by the concerns of Adam Smith on the value of diamonds and water. Smith is widely considered the father of economics, but he struggled to understand why diamonds were so expensive when they were not important to everyday life. By contrast water is essential, but the price is usually much cheaper. This became known as the paradox of value and it has quite a simple explanation. Smith failed to distinguish between the total value of diamonds and the marginal value. In our lifetime, we may purchase only one or two diamonds. The marginal value of buying one diamond wedding ring is very high. However, when we have one diamond ring, the marginal value quickly falls. By contrast, after purchasing one unit of water, the marginal value of water will be exactly the same the next day. Therefore, we are buying water that is essential to life every day, so the total value of water in our lifetime is much higher than diamonds, which we may buy only irregularly. Because diamonds are scarce, firms can command a high price. Firms can also take advantage of our willingness to pay a high price for diamonds for these special occasions.

8
Diminishing Returns

Diminishing returns refers to the fact that increasing consumption can lead to a fall in marginal utility.

As mentioned in the previous topic, our first bar of chocolate gives substantial satisfaction, but the second will give much less enjoyment. In this case, the law of diminishing returns begins after the first bar of chocolate. It is why our personal demand curve will be downward sloping. This is likely to be true for many goods we purchase. For the first unit, we are willing to pay a high price, because we get strong utility from it. But if a second unit gives us very little utility, we would value the good far less and therefore not want to pay the market price.

DIMINISHING RETURNS IN PRODUCTION

Diminishing returns does not just occur in consumption; a firm will also face diminishing returns in the short term when it tries to produce more goods. Suppose a farmer has a fixed quantity of land. Using more fertilizer will enable the farmer to increase output. The first quantity of fertilizer may be able to increase output by 20%, as the extra nutrients make a big difference. However, the same quantity of fertilizer used shortly afterwards will offer an increase in output that will be significantly less, say 5%. This is because there are only so many nutrients that a plant needs or can absorb. In other words, using fertilizers quickly has diminishing returns. Fertilizers can increase output, but it doesn't mean more fertilizers are always desirable. To increase output will require the farmer to look at other methods.

DIMINISHING RETURNS

A key feature of diminishing returns in production is that one factor of production must be fixed. If a tea shop wants to increase its capacity for selling tea, it can employ more workers. With more waiters, it can serve more customers. However, there comes a point where employing extra

Waiters in the café: there are only so many extra workers it is worth employing.

waiters starts to have diminishing returns. There is limited space in the café, and many workers will start to get in each other's way. The fifth or sixth worker will enable the tea shop to sell more cups of tea, but the increase in output will be significantly less than the cups of tea sold by the first two or three workers.

An important factor is that in the long term, the firm could avoid diminishing returns by building a bigger café, expanding the number of tables and serving area. With a bigger café, that sixth worker will no longer be experiencing diminishing returns because the basic infrastructure of the café is different. A bigger café could still face diminishing returns, but it may not start to occur until the tenth or eleventh worker.

IMPLICATIONS OF DIMINISHING RETURNS

If extra workers create diminishing returns, and produce only a few extra cups of tea, then the marginal cost of increasing output will increase. If a worker costs £10 an hour but increases orders by only two cups of tea, the marginal cost of those cups of tea is £5. If the first worker also costs £10 an hour but achieves orders of 20 cups of tea, the marginal cost of those cups of tea is £0.50. Therefore, the firm faces a very different cost structure. Early on, selling tea is very cheap. But the fifth worker is very inefficient and extra cups of tea cost £5.00 – making it uneconomic to produce more tea.

There are many areas of life where diminishing returns can occur, without us necessarily being aware of them. If we are revising for an exam, the first two hours will be most effective, but if we stay up late in the night, trying to cram more information, the extra hours will have a lower reward and diminishing returns from our effort.

DIMINISHING RETURNS OF MONEY

Another important application of diminishing returns is in income and wealth. If you have no money, earning £1,000 will be vital to improving your living standards, so the utility is very significant. However, if you are earning £50,000 a year, an extra £1,000 will have a much smaller increase in utility. It is still welcome and you can spend it on treats like takeaways, suggesting that there is some increase in utility, but it is significantly less than the happiness from the first £1,000. For a millionaire, an extra £1,000 will have a negligible impact on utility. With an income of £1 million, an extra £1,000 may even have no discernible effect on living standards. It may be hard to think of anything to buy with this extra money. There will be some increase in utility – even if it is a slight happiness at seeing more money in the bank – but we can see how there are very strong diminishing returns, the more money that we get.

Diminishing returns

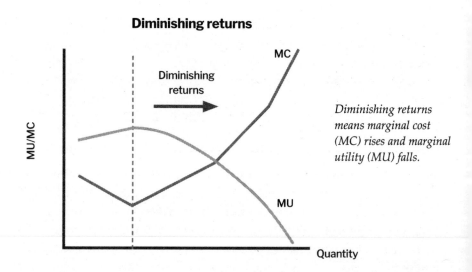

Diminishing returns means marginal cost (MC) rises and marginal utility (MU) falls.

This is a strong justification for a progressive taxation system. Taking an extra £1,000 from a millionaire reduces their utility by only a small amount. Giving a small amount to the poor has a significant increase in utility. Therefore, redistributing income within society can increase total utility and total satisfaction – even though the amount of income stays the same.

Now this argument has its critics: some argue that too much progressive taxation reduces incentives and the rich may not work and create income in the first place. But, although this can be true to an extent, the diminishing returns from wealth and income do mean a highly unequal society, and one in which wealth is not used efficiently to maximize overall social happiness.

9
The Free Market

A free market refers to an economy characterized by the voluntary exchange of goods and services, with little or no intervention by the government.

In a free market, firms and consumers are free to decide what to produce, what price to set and how much to buy. Therefore, a free market is self-regulating and does not have any external government coercion such as regulation, taxation or price control. The attraction of a free market is that, even if people act out of self-interest, this will contribute to the general good. As Adam Smith noted:

> *It is not from the benevolence of the butcher, the brewer or the baker, that we expect our dinner, but from their regard to their own self-interest.*

The Wealth of Nations (1776)

By seeking profit, firms provide the goods that consumers need and want. If firms become inefficient, they will lose out to other firms who are able to offer better products. Therefore, this 'survival of the fittest' ensures that all firms face an incentive to continually innovate, invest and operate for the lowest cost. In the long term, this creates a dynamic and efficient economy, which promotes economic growth and development. Some economies

Adam Smith.

have experimented with the opposite of free markets – such as central planning where governments decide what to produce – but these alternative systems tend to have long-term limitations and inevitable inefficiencies and wastage, so in practice most economies have a degree of free markets.

CLASSICAL FREE MARKETS

To early classical economists like Adam Smith, a free market implies the absence of monopoly power and producers who are competitive. Smith believed that a firm with monopoly power is able to charge higher prices and exploit customers and/or workers. The absence of competition means that there is not a truly free exchange of goods and services, so the market may require government intervention to avoid exploitation of both customers and workers.

LAISSEZ-FAIRE VIEW

A libertarian view of a free market is more closely associated with limited or no government intervention. In this view of a free market, the government would not intervene even if firms developed monopoly power. This is associated with the idea of laissez-faire economics (literally, free from intervention).

There is a close correlation between the free market and capitalism. Often the terms are used interchangeably – though there is a difference in focus. Capitalism is an economic system focusing on the private ownership of land, capital and business. Free market capitalism, therefore, requires government intervention to protect private property and the individual ownership of business, but the government then takes a 'hands-off' approach to the regulation of individual markets. Free-market capitalism is associated with economic efficiency and higher rates of growth, but in the complete absence of government regulation and taxes the outcome is liable to become highly unequal, with the owners of capital able to generate monopoly power and rent-seeking activity.

FREE-MARKET SOCIALIST VIEW

Some economists argue that a capitalist model doesn't lead to particularly free markets because monopoly owners can use their dominant market position to exclude rival firms and protect their monopoly profits. There is actually a free-market socialist view which states that markets should be left to market forces of supply and demand, though the ownership

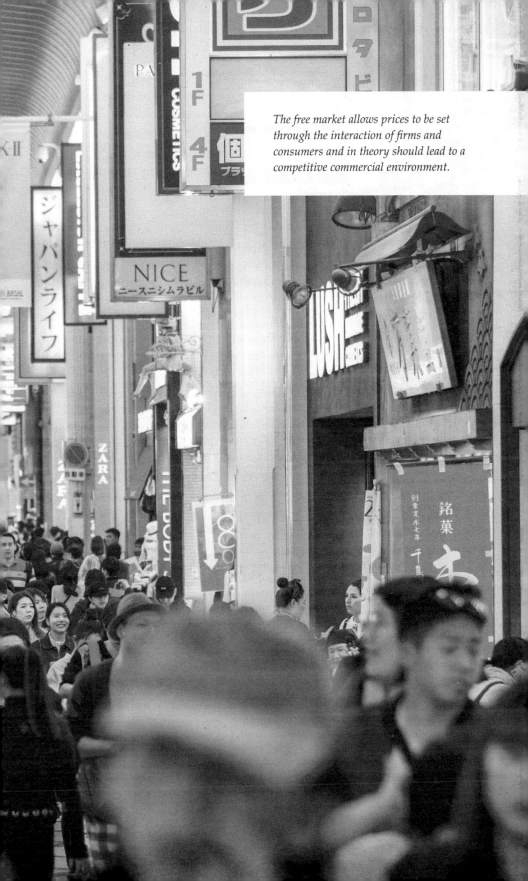

The free market allows prices to be set through the interaction of firms and consumers and in theory should lead to a competitive commercial environment.

of the means of production should not be in the hands of a limited number of capitalists but shared with the whole population. This would require firms to be either cooperatives or privately owned firms which have their profits taxed for spending on public goods. In this model, the markets operate freely, but the proceeds from the market activity are more equitably distributed. In other words, it is an attempt to have the advantages of free markets but remove the distortions of private property, inequality and monopoly power.

However, this view of a free market is criticized by other libertarian economists who argue that as soon as governments are involved in owning resources, the usual market incentives will be distorted and the government will inevitably start to intervene in the distribution of income and goods.

In practice, most economies have a mixture of free markets and government intervention. Where possible the distribution of goods is left to market forces, but the government often intervenes in regulating externalities, extreme inequality and providing public goods (such as health and education, which are underprovided by a free market).

10
Monopoly

Monopoly is a situation where one firm dominates the market. For example, tap water, train routes and Facebook.

A pure monopoly is a firm with 100% of the market, but in practice any firm with over 25% market share may be considered to have monopoly power. A firm with monopoly power is able to set higher prices, restrict supply and use its market power to pay low prices to suppliers and deter rivals. For understandable reasons, monopolies are viewed with suspicion and often regulated by governments, but despite the drawbacks monopolies can still be necessary for certain industries.

Most firms would crave monopoly power because it is a quick route to greater profitability. However, to gain monopoly power, there needs to be substantial barriers to entry. The most common barrier to entry comes from economies of scale, when a very large firm benefits from lower average costs, making it difficult for new firms to enter the industry. For example, in aerospace manufacture, there are very substantial fixed costs. Building a new aeroplane requires billions of dollars of investment. This is why the market is dominated by two main companies – Boeing and

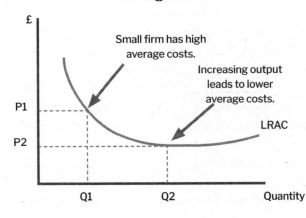

Average costs

A diagram showing economies of scale with falling long run average costs (LRAC).

Many different brands but owned by just a few big companies.

Airbus. It is difficult for new firms to enter because at a smaller scale, average costs would be much higher.

A successful modern monopoly is Amazon. It has such a high output that it is efficient to have its own very successful next-day delivery service. This is an example of how its monopoly power and high share of the market makes it difficult for other firms to compete. A new rival to Amazon would struggle to replicate the size and extent of the Amazon infrastructure, and therefore Amazon is able to maintain its monopoly power.

Other barriers to entry can include: a legal barrier to entry – e.g. government monopoly on letter delivery; geographical barriers – e.g. access to important commodities; and vertical integration – e.g. access to key supply chains. Many barriers to entry are beyond the control of a company, but a firm can create its own monopoly power through advertising and creating strong brand loyalty. For example, Unilever and Procter & Gamble have spent billions on advertising to create a powerful brand loyalty for different types of soap powder. They also use advertising to create an illusion of competition. For example, popular soap-powder brands – Ariel, Bold, Cheer, Daz, Dreft, Tide, Era – are all made by one company, Procter & Gamble. The advertising and brand loyalty to this range of products makes it more difficult for competitors to enter the market.

PROBLEM OF MONOPOLIES

The main problem of monopolies is that firms can exploit their market power to set higher prices. If your bill for tap water goes up, you have no alternative but to pay the price increases or lose access. If you commute to work by train every day, the firm has a captive market. Therefore, monopolies can maximize profits by squeezing consumers. This is particularly an issue for essential products, like gas, electricity and petrol. Furthermore, a firm with monopoly power, like a supermarket, is likely to also have monopoly buying power (called monopsony). This means that it can squeeze suppliers by paying a very low profit margin. For example, farmers have complained that large supermarkets are in a position to dictate the price they pay for food such as milk and butter. This monopoly means the supermarkets profit twice, buying from suppliers at a low price and selling to consumers at a high price. This highlights a major social concern of monopoly – it represents a redistribution of income from consumers and suppliers to the shareholders of the monopoly company, and increases inequality within society.

The postal service often runs as a monopoly

INEFFICIENCY OF MONOPOLY

Another potential problem of monopoly is that a firm that can easily make high profit may lack any incentive to cut costs, develop new products and offer good consumer service. For example, if a town has only one restaurant or one petrol station, then no matter what kind of service they offer, both have a captive market and will remain profitable. But, if they start to have competition from other firms, they will have a much greater incentive to offer better service and quality products to avoid losing customers. This is the logic behind a policy known as deregulation. In the past, there was just one supplier of electricity, gas and postal companies – a legal monopoly – but governments in the United States, United Kingdom and Europe wanted to introduce competition into these markets to encourage more efficiency and lower prices for consumers.

THE BENEFITS OF MONOPOLY

Monopolies understandably get a bad reputation, but there can be circumstances where they may be a 'necessary evil'. Take the drinking water industry, for example. With a remit to provide tap water to every home in the country, it would make sense to have only one firm and one set of infrastructure. For another firm to have a rival set of water pipes would be very wasteful and inefficient. Tap water, like electricity production and railways, are what economists describe as a 'natural monopoly' – an industry where the most efficient number of firms is one. Having more than one would lead to significantly higher costs. Even

Railways rarely can allow competition on the same tracks.

if a monopoly charges excess prices, it is better than having to pay for multiple networks.

Another advantage of monopoly is that very high profits can be used to invest in research and development. One example is energy companies, who are very profitable but, in theory, use some of this profit to invest in new renewable energy systems like wind farms. It is true a high share of profit may just be paid in dividends to shareholders, but equally, without the monopoly profit, there would be less investment in new forms of power generation, which will be important for the future.

Also, it is not necessarily the case that monopolies will be inefficient, like some claim. A firm may gain monopoly power precisely because they are innovative, dynamic and efficient. Modern monopolies like Google or Amazon have created products and services with which other firms struggle to compete. If the management structure is right, monopolies can continue to be efficient and dynamic.

11

Game Theory

Game theory involves examining decisions where there are multiple possible outcomes depending on how other people and firms act. Game theory is the art of strategy and has many applications in the domain of economics.

PRICE WAR

Suppose a firm is deciding what to do with its prices. A large petrol retailer may consider cutting prices to gain market share and therefore gain more profits. However, the decision about whether to cut prices or not depends on how its rivals react. If their rivals react to a price cut by keeping their prices the same, then the firm who initiated the price cut is likely to see a significant increase in profits, and the decision will be desirable. However, there is no guarantee that other firms will react by doing nothing. Those rivals may decide it is against their interests to lose market share and profits to the price cutter. Therefore they may

A price war (d) means much lower profits than stable prices (a)

		Firm B	
		Stable prices	Price war
Firm A	Stable prices	$40, $40 (a)	$0, $60 (b)
	Price war	$60, $0 (c)	$3, $3 (d)

Firms have to decide whether to try and keep stable prices or start a price war.

respond by cutting prices too. In this case, the outcome for the first firm is very different. They have lower prices, but gain no increase in market share, and so get less profits. When making a choice, it is therefore very important to know how rivals will respond.

In an oligopoly (a market structure dominated by a few firms), there is a temptation for the firms to collude and reach an agreement, where they increase prices and agree to restrict output. This collusion takes out the uncertainty of price setting because they are guaranteed a situation of higher prices without becoming uncompetitive because their rivals agree to the same price increase. This is the logic behind a cartel like OPEC. They wish to set the profit-maximizing price for the industry. OPEC is a global cartel, but for domestic markets, governments usually legislate against cartels and collusion because it is not in the public interest. If firms are found guilty of collusion, they can be given large fines, which diminish the incentive to collude.

NASH EQUILIBRIUM

A Nash equilibrium is a particular outcome in game theory, where no agent can get a better outcome by changing its decision. When there is Nash equilibrium, a firm is left with no regrets. A Nash equilibrium may involve two firms keeping prices stable. If one increased prices, it would lose market share and profitability. If one firm cut prices, it would start a price war and lose profitability. Therefore, the best choice for both firms is to keep prices stable. This is the best outcome given the choices faced. However, the Nash equilibrium isn't necessarily the best possible outcome. If both firms agree together to increase prices, this is even better (for the firms) than keeping prices stable. But, if you have no influence on your rival, the best choice is to keep prices stable.

GAME THEORY AND IRRATIONAL BEHAVIOUR

Game theory generally assumes that firms are rational and agents will take the decision which maximizes their utility (e.g. profit, satisfaction). However, in the real world, there may be several other factors to take into consideration. For example, a boss of a company may feel like doing something dramatic to get attention. They may start a price war because they want to, even if it leads to lower profits. Also, accepting lower profits may not be irrational but in fact maximize some other objective (in order eventually to maximize profit). A firm's goal may be to maximize market share – even if this leads to an initial loss. This

The city of Kyiv in March 2022. According to game theory, there is no reason to start a war – yet wars continue to happen.

is what Amazon did for many years – making an operating loss to gain an ever-increasing share of the market.

Another limitation of game theory is that it tends to ignore more altruistic motivations to cooperate or malevolent motivations to hurt others even if it hurts yourself. For example, war is incredibly expensive, especially in modern times, so according to game theory, there is no logic to starting a war. In February 2022, the president of Russia made that very choice.

TRADE WAR

In economic terms, an example of an illogical choice made despite game theory is a trade war. Free trade without tariffs would lead to the best outcome for both countries. However, a country may wish to start a trade war even though it leads to a loss of overall economic welfare.

REPEATED GAMES

Also, when looking at game theory, it depends whether the strategy is for a one-off game or a game that is repeated many times. For example, if a new firm enters a market, it may decide to set low prices as it wishes to gain market share. In the short term, the incumbent firm responds by cutting prices too. Therefore, for a short time period, consumers get the benefit of lower prices. However, over time, firms in the market learn that if they steadily increase price, their profitability rises and that price wars are counterproductive. Therefore, the longer firms are competing against each other, the more they tend to find ways to avoid damaging price wars. Some firms may promise to 'price match' – if you find the good cheaper elsewhere, they will refund you the difference. While it may sound great for consumers, it is actually a clever way for firms to discourage price wars. What a firm is saying to its rival is: if you cut prices, we will cut them by exactly the same, so there is no point!

12
Pricing Strategies

How do firms go about setting prices? Why do airline flights change price from day to day? Are promises to price match rivals as good as they sound?

Firstly, when setting prices a firm will have different motivations; they may wish to maximize profits or they may wish to maximize market share. For example, for several years, the pricing strategy of Amazon was dominated by a wish to develop market penetration. It kept prices as low as possible in order to gain market share and loyal repeat customers. For several years, it made zero profit but was constantly expanding, and it came to dominate online selling. Once its dominance was well established, it was able to change its pricing strategy and increase its profit margins.

MARKET STRUCTURE
Another key factor that will determine pricing strategy is the market structure that a firm faces. If the market is very competitive and consumers have innumerable choices, a firm will have no alternative but to set quite low prices in order not to lose market share. However, at the other end of the spectrum, a firm with monopoly power will find it much easier to increase prices and take advantage of the inelastic demand. If a firm

Ink cartridges are usually more profitable than the printer.

with monopoly power like Apple or a local train company increases prices, many consumers will keep buying.

DIFFERENT TYPES OF STRATEGIES

Apart from basic pricing strategies, there are numerous ways that firms can attract customers and increase profits. Sometimes, firms will offer products at a very low rate to attract customers into the shop. For example, a supermarket offering a can of baked beans for 7p will make headline news (it happened in 1994), gaining lots of attention and potentially new customers who come for the cheap baked beans but end up buying many other items too. This is known as a loss leader – selling some goods at a loss to make profit elsewhere. A similar example is printers and ink. You can buy a good printer for £50, which appears very cheap, but to buy ink cartridges for the cheap printer can easily cost you £25. No prizes for guessing where printer companies make their profit.

At the other extreme, some firms may make use of high prices to reinforce the idea of a premium product. For example, by selling very expensive premium wine, a restaurant may give itself the impression of a high-end restaurant, and the customer can feel they are getting a good deal by buying a cheaper house wine.

PRICE DISCRIMINATION

One great challenge firms have when setting prices is that every customer is different. Some customers have bottomless pockets and are unfazed by a rise in prices; others are very price conscious and a small rise in prices may cause them to look elsewhere for better value. This is why some firms will attempt to separate their market into different segments and charge different groups of people different prices. At its most basic, a 10% discount might be offered to students or pensioners. The logic is simple: this group of people have lower incomes and will be responsive to a lower price. If the firm cut prices 10% for everyone, it would lose revenue, but by cutting prices just for the target groups it increases sales to students and pensioners and maintains relatively high prices for everyone else.

Wine may be priced highly to emphasize that it is a premium product.

Price discrimination

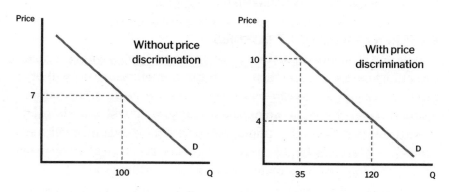

Price discrimination means selling the same good at different prices.

Not every firm can engage in price discrimination, which requires a degree of market power and the ability to separate markets. The ideal for firms would be to discriminate prices depending on income, but this is not practical, which is why generic groupings such as age are used. Another way to price discriminate is on the quantity of a good. For example, when buying gas or electricity, the first 100 or so units are quite expensive, but for higher quantities the price tends to be lower. This is because the first 100 units are essential (our demand is inelastic), but for more quantity, we could find substitutes or not use the electricity (our demand is elastic). The gas and electric companies use these pricing strategies to maximize their revenue.

Related to price discrimination is dynamic pricing, a strategy that has been increasingly used in recent years by airlines and even train companies. It is a sophisticated way to set prices, which can respond to every change in market demand. The airline seeks to maximize revenue by selling all the tickets for a flight at the highest prices possible. However, if a flight is not popular, prices will fall, encouraging more demand. If a flight becomes very popular and could sell out soon, the prices will be increased so that only those willing to pay the very high prices get the last tickets for the flight. When booking a flight, you will probably notice that the most unsociable hours for flying – 6 a.m. and 11 p.m. – are the cheapest. This is simply dynamic pricing in action. Peak hour travel is more desirable, so prices rise as the tickets sell quickly.

Another modified form of price discrimination is known as price skimming. This occurs when a popular company brings out a new product. If the product is in high demand, the firm may charge a high price as the super-keen buyers are willing to pay the high price. However, over time, the firm will have to reduce the price if it wants to sell to a wider customer base who will buy only if they feel it is good value and competitive. Examples include items like the latest models of X-Box and iPhone.

It is quite common for a firm to promise to price match their nearest rival – if you see this elsewhere, we will refund the difference. It sounds a great deal for consumers. But, it can be a way to discourage price competition amongst firms. If your rival has a price match scheme, you have little incentive to cut prices because your rival is committed to doing the same. Therefore, it is in the interests of all firms to keep prices stable, and not start a price war – because your rival has made a highly publicized promise to follow suit. Therefore, because both firms know they will lose from a price war, they don't start one – and as a bonus, the customer thinks they are getting a good deal!

Each seat can have different values for different customers and therefore the price varies.

13

Elasticity

Elasticity measures the responsiveness of demand to a change in price or income. Understanding how elastic or inelastic a good is can have a crucial effect on setting prices and in explaining consumer behaviour.

We would expect a higher price to cause a fall in demand, but the question is: how much will demand fall? This is what elasticity measures. If the prices go up, which goods will you keep buying and for which products will you seek alternatives?

Suppose the price of petrol increases 10%, and demand falls only 1%, we say that demand is price inelastic – demand is relatively unresponsive to the change in price. By contrast, suppose the price of a Fiat Punto increased 10%, demand for that particular car may fall by 15%. A car buyer has quite a few alternative cars to buy, but if the price of petrol goes up, all those with petrol cars have no alternative but to keep buying.

INELASTIC DEMAND

We say a good has inelastic demand when an increase in price leads to a smaller percentage fall in demand.

Goods which are inelastic tend to have few alternatives and little competition. They are also goods which are necessary or essential – something we cannot do without. If we are addicted to tobacco, a higher price for cigarettes does not stop us smoking, so the demand is quite inelastic.

$$\text{Price Elasticity of Demand (PED)} \quad = \quad \frac{\text{\% change in Quantity Demanded}}{\text{\% change in Price}}$$

ELASTIC DEMAND

A good is price elastic when a change in price causes a bigger percentage change in demand.

Goods which are sensitive to price changes are those goods which typically have many alternatives. If you are buying soap powder, a higher price for one brand will encourage you to switch. If the price of pineapples increases, most consumers would prefer to switch to other types of fruit. Also, if the good is a large percentage of your income, such as a foreign holiday, a higher price may make it unaffordable, meaning demand will be quite price elastic.

WHY DOES ELASTICITY MATTER?

A firm would like their demand to be price inelastic, which will enable them to increase price without losing too many consumers and therefore become more profitable. Why do Coca-Cola spend billions every year on advertising? To make demand for Coca-Cola price inelastic. Strong brand loyalty means most consumers do not want to switch to an alternative. If the price is more expensive than supermarket own brand cola, consumers still buy the more expensive Coca-Cola.

Another related concept is the taxes on cigarettes and alcohol. Why are governments keen on increasing them? Partly because they are seen as 'demerit' or 'sin' goods. But also it is their inelastic demand. If the government increases tax on cigarettes, there tends to be only a small fall in demand. Most of the tax is passed onto the consumer and so the government sees a large rise in tax revenue.

ELASTICITY OVER TIME

Suppose the price of natural gas rises 50%, how will that affect demand? Most consumers will cut back on some consumption (turning down gas central heating), but generally, they are captive, needing gas for cooking and heating. A price rise of 50% may lead to a fall in demand of 10% – making the good quite price inelastic (-0.2). However, this is the short-term effect. In the long term,

Coca-Cola is price inelastic due to strong brand loyalty.

Consumers queue up outside an Apple store. Brand loyalty can make a product price inelastic.

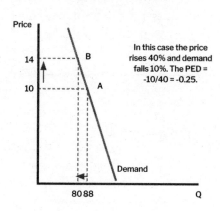

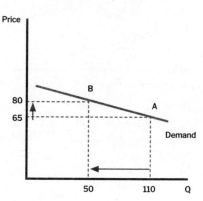

consumers may make efforts to find a cheaper alternative. If the price rise has lasted for a few years, consumers needing to buy a new cooker may now choose an electric oven. They may even switch from gas-powered hot water to an electric heat pump. Obviously it is a big investment to spend £3,000 on a new central heating system, but if the gas price rises are large enough, the demand for gas may start to fall over time.

This may have an importance for firms. For example, when Netflix started, they dominated the market for streaming TV. Demand was inelastic, and when they increased the price, the market kept growing. However, there comes a point where raising the price encourages more competitors to enter the streaming market and, eventually, consumers will give up on Netflix and move to cheaper alternatives. This shows elasticity matters: in the short term, demand may be inelastic, but this is not guaranteed to last.

Tomatoes, like most raw food, have an inelastic supply as they take several months to grow.

ELASTICITY OF SUPPLY

The concept of elasticity can be extended to other branches of economics like the elasticity of supply. If the price of a good rises, how much will firms increase supply?

If they increase by only a small percentage, we say supply is price inelastic. If supply increases by a bigger percentage, we say supply is price elastic. A key factor is the difficulty or ease of a firm increasing supply. For example, if the price of beer increases, it is relatively easy for firms to expand production and meet the increased demand. However, if the price of diamonds increases, it is much harder to increase supply, because there is only a limited quantity and to find a new source of diamonds and build a new mine takes a long time.

IMPORTANCE OF ELASTICITY OF SUPPLY

In agriculture the supply of raw food items is inelastic, at least in the short term. A crop may take four to six months from sowing to harvest. So even if the price of tomatoes rises rapidly, farmers cannot respond to this for a few months. This can make the price of agricultural products quite volatile. High prices encourage more supply, but by the time the extra supply comes onto the market, there is a glut and prices drop. This may cause farmers to cut back on supply, causing prices to rise again.

INCOME ELASTICITY OF DEMAND

If your income grows, what goods will you buy more of? Probably the luxury goods – foreign holidays, organic food, expensive wine. When income is low, you can't justify spending money on these, but when income rises, a bigger percentage of income will go here. Some basic or 'inferior' goods may even see a fall in demand. If your income rises, you buy organic sourdough bread and so stop buying supermarket own brand 'value' bread. Demand for organic bread is income elastic. Demand for value bread can have a negative income elasticity of demand (higher income leads to lower demand).

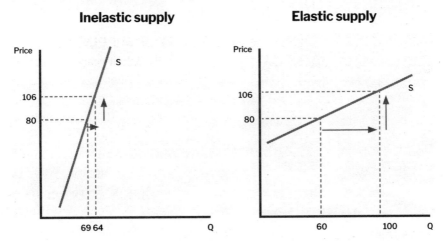

14
Supply-side Policies

Supply-side policies are government reforms to promote a more efficient and productive economy.

There are two main approaches to supply-side policies. The first could be termed market-oriented because they are reforms that try to harness the efficiencies and incentives of the free market. The second are termed interventionist because they seek to deal with market failure and rely on government intervention to improve the productive capacity of the economy. Free-market supply-side policies became popular in the 1980s in both the United Kingdom and United States as Prime Minister Thatcher and President Reagan were sympathetic to the idea of reducing the reach of governments and unleashing the potential of the market.

FREE-MARKET SUPPLY-SIDE POLICIES
A major supply-side policy is privatization. This involves selling state-owned companies to private buyers. The logic is that government

Ronald Reagan.

The 1984 miners' strike.

ownership of a firm or industry means there is a lack of a profit incentive, and the firm tends to become stagnant and unresponsive. A government-owned firm is too big to fail, but managers lack the ruthlessness to cut costs and innovate. When firms are privatized, the incentive of maximizing profits will encourage firms to cut costs. There is mixed evidence on the privatization of state-owned firms. In some industries, such as telecoms and airlines (helped by technology), there have been significant falls in prices and a new range of products and pricing strategies. Privatization has been more controversial for an industry like water, which is a natural monopoly (because there is no effective competition). In this case, privatization swaps a state-owned monopoly for a private monopoly and requires government regulation, otherwise the private firm can exploit consumers with higher prices.

The effect of supply-side policies

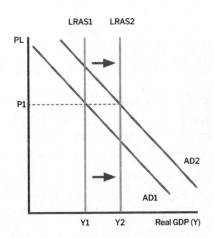

LRAS = long run aggregate supply
AD = aggregate demand

Another key supply-side policy is deregulation or competitive tendering. The aim is to end monopoly power and make firms face competition. Supporters argue that this is the best way to drive down prices and encourage firms to offer better service. Where industries do become genuinely more competitive, consumers tend to benefit from lower prices because monopoly power invariably leads to higher prices. Deregulation often accompanies privatization to avoid the creation of private monopolies.

Another key supply-side policy is the deregulation of labour markets. This can involve reducing the power of trade unions, reducing minimum wages and removing legislation that protects workers, by making it hard to fire them, say, or instituting a maximum working week. The idea is that more flexible labour markets will reduce costs for firms, making them more willing to hire workers in the first place. Margaret Thatcher, in particular, felt that trade unions were blocking productivity growth by stifling new working practices. More flexible labour markets are understandably supported by employers but criticized by workers. But this is a balancing act: labour market regulations can help protect workers against unscrupulous employers, and pushing low wages and a lack of rights can lead to a low wage economy with less investment in productivity. Countries with high wages need to adapt with higher productivity.

Another popular but contentious supply-side policy is that of tax cuts. The logic is that cutting income tax and corporation tax will help boost labour supply and business investment. If workers get to keep a higher share of their income, tax cuts may create an incentive for workers to do overtime and work harder. If tax rates rise to 70 or 80%, the incentive for overtime or working longer is reduced. Similarly, if there is a cut in corporation tax, the firm can retain more profit to use for investment, which will increase the productive capacity of the economy in the long run. There are times when tax cuts can boost productivity. When France experimented with a marginal tax rate of 85% for millionaires, the increase in tax revenue was very limited because many of the wealthy moved to other European countries with lower tax rates. In this case, lower taxes would provide an incentive to work harder. However, if you take the UK and US, where marginal tax rates are lower at 30–40%, cutting tax rates has minimal effect.

On the one hand, lower tax rates increase the incentive to work rather than take time off, but on the other hand, a worker can reach his target income by working fewer hours. In practice, most workers don't have much ability to change their weekly hours in response to tax changes. The case with corporation tax is similar. In the post-war period, corporation tax rates around the world were much higher, but investment was quite strong and economic growth high. However, in recent decades there has been significant tax competition as countries try to offer lower corporation tax rates to attract investment. Companies have benefitted from falling corporation tax rates, but overall investment is not significantly higher.

INTERVENTIONIST SUPPLY-SIDE POLICIES

Another approach to supply-side policies is trying to provide public goods that are underprovided in a free market. For example, a country's economic growth may be hampered by a lack of ports and transport links. To overcome these barriers may require central planning and investment from the government to provide better transport links, which is essentially a public good from which the whole economy benefits. There is a similar logic to investing in education and better training. A firm may be reluctant to invest in general training, because after they have spent the money, the worker could go and work elsewhere. But, if the government provides improved apprenticeships and training

Supply-side Policies

Free-market oriented	Interventionist
Privatization – sell state-owned assets to private sector – improve incentives	Public sector investment in infrastructure – improve transportation and reduce costs
Deregulation – allow new firms to enter the market – open monopolies to competition	Education – increase funding to schools and universities – improve labour productivity
Income tax cuts – greater incentive to work longer hours	Vocational training – government schemes to provide new skills to those who lose jobs
Flexible labour markets – reduce power of trade unions, minimum wages and regulations	Housing supply – increase supply of council housing – improves geographical mobility
Free-trade agreements – reduce tariff barriers and other obstacles to trade	Health spending – public spending on health can reduce hours lost to ill health
Reduce welfare benefits – increase the incentive to get a job	

for jobs where there is a shortage of workers, this can help to increase overall labour productivity.

Supply-side policies are generally quite popular, because in theory, they can increase economic growth, reduce inflation and unemployment, and improve international competitiveness. If successful, there are no real downsides, only a stronger economy. The only drawback is that it is difficult for any government supply-side policy to be really successful. The greatest leaps in productivity (with the exception of wartime) have tended to come from private sector innovation and invention of new working practices, from the assembly line to transistors and the microchip. Also, even the best supply-side policies will take a long time to have any effect. You can't improve labour skills overnight. This time lag can be frustrating and also makes it difficult to evaluate their success. The other crucial aspect of supply-side policies is that it depends how they are implemented. There is a huge difference between privatizing an industry like the railways or healthcare and privatizing the steel industry. A profit motive is less important for motivating workers in healthcare and education.

Constructing ports is an example of using supply-side policies to overcome the lack of provision of public goods in a free market economy.

15

Incentives

Incentives are a crucial element of a market economy. It is the incentive of profit which encourages an entrepreneur to take a risk and set up a business.

It is the incentive of higher pay which encourages a worker to do overtime. Without incentives, economies become moribund and stagnant. One of the big differences between a market economy and a planned economy is that planned economies usually lack any real incentives. If your income or profit is the same no matter how much you work, it is unsurprising if firms make little effort to cut costs.

Incentives are also an important cog in the invisible hand of the market. Suppose there is growth in demand for streaming TV channels. How does the market react to this change in consumer behaviour? Well, the growth in demand means companies can sell TV programmes for a higher price to companies like Netflix and Amazon. This higher price will encourage more investment and higher salaries for actors. Rather than take a part in a blockbuster film, actors and directors will find a higher

The Oil Shock of 1973 led countries to search for new sources of oil.

return from making TV series for companies like Netflix. Without any external direction, the higher demand and price for streaming TV shows has created incentives for companies to enter the market for producing suitable programmes. On the other hand, as the demand for going out to the cinema falls, cinema firms will notice a fall in profit and there will be an incentive to find a more profitable use of their prime real estate which reflects changing consumer behaviour.

What happens if there is a fall in the supply of oil due to an oil embargo or cutting off supplies from a major supplier? In this case, the price will rise and consumers will be faced with much higher prices. However, this short-term change in the market is not the end of the story. When the price of oil rises, it creates an incentive for firms to find new oil supplies or alternative sources of energy. For example, in the 1970s, the supply of oil was dominated by OPEC countries in the Middle East. But, when the price of oil tripled in 1973, this created a very significant incentive for countries around the world to look at whether they could produce oil – even in places where doing so is more costly. When the price of oil goes over $100 a barrel, it becomes profitable to produce oil even in remote places like the Arctic, which has high costs of extraction. Therefore, the Oil Shock of 1973 led to a paradoxical weakening of OPEC – the high price they had engineered created an incentive for new countries to produce oil and the supply of oil become more diversified.

An important caveat is that incentives can take considerable time to work. For example, in 2022, there was a sharp rise in the price of natural gas, due to both rising oil prices and the Ukraine war. However, even though the price of natural gas increased seven-fold over previous levels, there is no easy fix to increasing supply. It takes time to build the infrastructure and gas pipes to create new sources of gas. There are incentives but also significant time delays. Also, there are some products where incentives may not be enough. For example, the price of renting in many city centres has grown exponentially. In a free market, this should create an incentive to increase the supply of housing. However, there may be either a shortage of land or restrictions on building, which mean the usual incentives do not apply, leading to continued shortage.

Less dramatic but perhaps more important for global poverty was the 2022 rise in the price of wheat. A fall in supply from both Ukraine and Russia caused record price levels of wheat – having significant implications for countries that rely on wheat imports. The good thing about wheat is that it can be grown in a wide variety of countries and from two sowings per year. Therefore, farmers will be constantly looking at the price of foodstuffs when deciding what to grow. A record price of wheat will definitely encourage farmers around the world to sow more wheat – to take advantage of the higher prices. For example, Indian farmers who traditionally do not sow wheat, will consider growing the crop when prices rise.

The higher price of wheat will also create all kinds of different incentives elsewhere in the economy. Farmers may stop growing crops for biofuels, and grow wheat instead. Also if wheat becomes substantially more expensive, this creates an incentive for consumers to find alternatives in their diet. For example, in Morocco and Algeria (both big importers of wheat), the higher wheat prices are very impactful on consumers used to eating breads and wheat-based products. If the wheat price remains high, they may decide to alter their diet – choosing other grains, such as rice, barley, corn and oats.

Record prices often make headline news. Less newsworthy is the almost unseen effect of incentives bringing markets back into equilibrium by creating the necessary conditions to increase supply or produce and consume other products. True, there are time delays and market incentives may not always work comprehensively, but it is incentives that are constantly helping land, labour and capital to be moved to the most efficient use in the economy.

The importance of incentives can have implications for economic policy. Suppose there is a long-term rise in gas prices due to supplies becoming scarce. A government may be tempted to subsidize prices to protect consumers, but these artificially low prices will take away the incentives of firms and consumers to switch to alternative energy supplies and this will only exacerbate the shortage of gas in the long term. Sometimes higher prices are a necessary response to prolonged shortages.

A high price for wheat may incentivize farmers to grow wheat instead of other crops.

16
Price Controls

In certain circumstances a government may wish to limit the increase in prices. For example, if food prices or rents increase too fast, the government may be concerned this would lead to poverty and decide therefore to set legal maximum limits on prices.

The advantage of price controls is that they can protect the poorest in society from unaffordable prices. They can also be used in an attempt to avoid excess inflationary pressures. If a government feels firms are price gouging, using their monopoly power to increase their profit margins, price controls can be a way to try and combat this abuse of market power.

PROBLEMS OF PRICE CONTROLS
In theory, price controls are an attractive policy for dealing with the twin problems of inflation and poverty. However, in practice, they will create unintended consequences that usually lead to a different kind of

Price controls

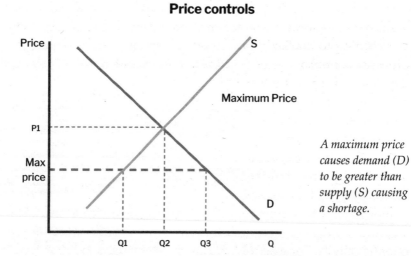

A maximum price causes demand (D) to be greater than supply (S) causing a shortage.

A price controls poster from the USA in World War II.

problem. Firstly, prices that are rising rapidly are indicative of a shortage of the good and/or excess demand. Imposing a price control doesn't deal with this fundamental problem. In fact, if there is a shortage of food, price controls could even make the situation worse. A lower price creates less incentive for suppliers to deal with the problem by increasing supply. So in the long term, price controls can lead to a prolonged shortage of food. Allowing prices to rise will create the market incentive for farmers to grow more food that will deal with the shortages.

Take, for another example, the shortage of gas in 2022. Many governments responded by capping prices. However, a problem is that if price controls keep prices artificially low, consumers will have less incentive to reduce demand. Therefore, the price cap could lead to a shortage of gas at the most critical point. If prices are allowed to rise according to market forces, this will encourage households and businesses to improve energy efficiency and find ways to get by with lower demand. These higher prices may be painful to households, but they do tackle the underlying issue of gas shortages. If the government is concerned about equity issues, a more efficient policy is to allow prices to rise but to give direct income support to those who need it most. In this way the government can achieve the best of both worlds – protect the living standards of the poorest but also retain market incentives to cut demand.

Another issue with price controls is that keeping prices artificially low will create shortages and a need for rationing. This will lead to wasteful economic activity. For example, during the 1970s Oil Shock, the United

States attempted price controls on petrol, and the result was long queues of cars waiting to get the limited supplies. If we spend one hour to get a good with a maximum price, we do have to factor in the additional cost of time. The petrol might be $4 a gallon, but if our hourly wage is $20, the true price of purchasing that petrol is $24. Price controls that distort the market will also invariably create a black market for illegal sales. With prices kept below the market equilibrium, those who can get the limited product are able to sell at higher price to those who would like to buy but were unable to get the limited supply. For example, with ticket prices for big concerts, there is always an inclination towards creating a black market for the reselling of tickets.

Price controls were tried during World War II in both the UK and US. By the end of the war, there were 15,000 employees working in the administration of price controls in the US, setting prices but also describing which goods were included and then enforcing those rules. This highlights the bureaucratic and inefficient nature of price controls. Furthermore, studies on this period suggest that output was 7% less than it otherwise would have been because the lower prices distorted the usual profit incentives.

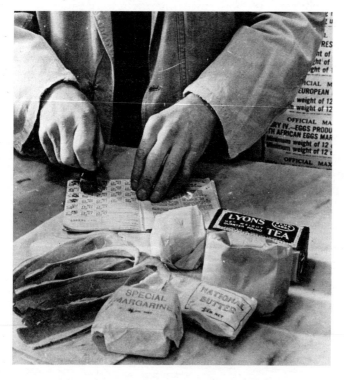

Food rationing in the UK in 1943.

OTHER REASONS FOR PRICE CONTROLS

Despite all the drawbacks of price controls, it is still possible to offer other justifications. For example, firms with very powerful monopoly power are able to increase prices because buyers have no alternatives. For example, if renters face a monopoly landlord increasing prices, they will find it difficult to switch accommodation. In this case, price controls may be introduced, but will have a very limited impact on reducing the supply of rented accommodation because supply is very inelastic. Landlords don't have many alternatives to letting out property, and the price controls merely reduce their excess profits.

To be effective, price controls really need some kind of rationing system or corresponding effort to increase supply. For example, in the two World Wars, the UK introduced price controls but also ration cards. This combination of ration books and price controls kept prices below equilibrium for a considerable time. Research suggests that the price controls did help to keep a lid on inflation in both the US and UK, but at the cost of very extensive government intervention, with large-scale bureaucracy and rationing. In peacetime, governments rarely have the stomach to keep price controls for too long because they require so much additional government intervention. In 1971 and 1973 President Nixon introduced price controls in a bid to reduce inflation, but these provided only temporary relief: the underlying inflationary pressures built, and inflation accelerated shortly after they were removed.

17

Inflation

Inflation is the phenomenon of rising prices – an increase in the cost of living. It is an economic concept that everybody will notice and which can seriously impact an individual's economic welfare.

High inflation can lead to uncertainty, and in its worst cases make normal economic activity unpalatable. It can wipe out savings, redistributing income from savers to borrowers. However, the impact of inflation will depend on a few factors. For example, what is the cause? Is it temporary? Are wages keeping up with rising prices?

There are two quite different causes of inflation. The first cause of inflation is when the economy is growing very quickly and the strong demand leads to shortages. In response to a shortage of goods and workers,

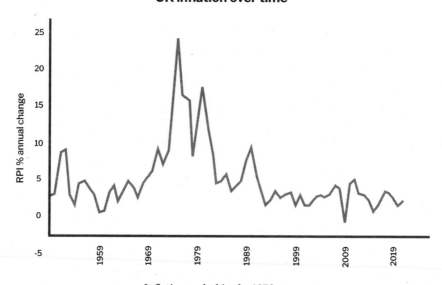

Inflation peaked in the 1970s.

firms respond by putting up prices and wages. For example, in the late 1980s, the United Kingdom (UK) experienced rapid economic growth due to rising real wages, high consumer confidence and government tax cuts. The UK economy grew at over 4% a year. This contrasted with a typical growth rate of 2.5%. It meant that demand for goods was rising faster than firms could supply them. The result was an increase in imports and rising prices. It was a classic example of an economic boom and we call this type of inflation demand-pull because prices are pulled up by higher demand.

A very different cause of inflation is called cost-push. This is when prices rise due to an increase in the cost of production. For example, rising oil prices often cause inflation. When oil prices rise, the cost of fuel increases as does the cost of transporting most goods in the economy. Consumers will face the rising price of petrol and firms will face higher transport costs and higher energy bills. In 1973, OPEC tripled the price of oil, setting off worldwide inflation, which reached over 20% in the United Kingdom and over 15% in the United States. In 2021/22, we had a new experience of cost-push inflation. The inflation of 2022 is caused by higher oil prices and higher gas prices, partly exacerbated by the conflict in Ukraine and sanctions on Russian oil/gas. There were also higher costs due to COVID lockdowns, which disrupted the usual supply chains. Ships were stuck in certain ports, which made shipping goods around the world more difficult and expensive. This contributed to global inflation.

For the average consumer, the cause of inflation is of little concern, but there is an important difference for policymakers. If inflation is caused by the economy growing too quickly, central banks can increase interest rates to slow down the rate of economic growth. Higher rates increase the cost of borrowing and will lead to lower consumer spending and investment. This will lead to a slower rate of economic growth and firms will be able to keep up with rising demand. This enables us – at least in theory – to reduce inflation without serious costs.

There are two further points to consider. If inflation is caused by strong economic growth, then wages are likely to be rising too. If your take home pay rises by 10%, and inflation is 7%, you are still seeing an increase in real wage of 3% a year. In this case, the costs of inflation are much lower. Also, when interest rates are higher than the inflation rate, then savers (who usually lose out from inflation) will instead find that the real value of their savings is protected.

Causes of inflation

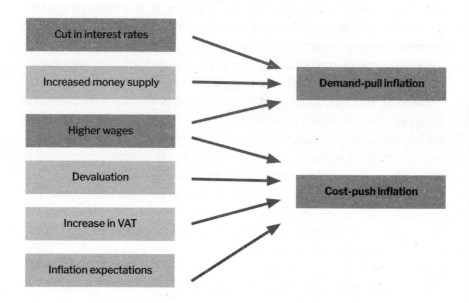

However, what happens when there is cost-push inflation, due to higher oil prices or a rise in import prices? The problem here is that not only do we have higher prices but we may have lower economic growth too. Higher oil prices reduce disposable incomes. Firms and consumers have to spend more on buying goods, but their income may not be keeping up. Prices are rising because of higher costs, but people do not feel better off because wages are not keeping up and real incomes are falling. This is something known as stagflation (see pages 89–92) – higher prices and lower economic growth, the worst of both worlds.

A central bank can increase interest rates to reduce inflation, but the higher rates will cause even lower economic growth. During the Global Financial Crisis of 2008, there was inflation of 5% and a recession at the same time. Central banks around the world cut interest rates to 0.5%. This meant savers became worse off and many workers saw a fall in real wages because inflation was higher than their wage growth. In 2022, many central banks faced a similar dilemma – raise interest rates to reduce inflation, but risk causing recession. It's a tricky balancing act.

WINNERS AND LOSERS OF INFLATION

Another feature of inflation is that it creates winners and losers. One of the potential winners from inflation is people who have borrowed a lot of money, such as a national government with very high levels of government debt. Why does a government benefit? During inflation, government revenue will rise because inflation will lead to higher nominal wages and higher levels of profit, meaning that the government receives higher income tax and higher sales tax. At the same time, the real value of the government bonds it sold to finance its deficit is falling. With higher nominal revenue, people who bought government bonds see a fall in the real value of their savings, making it easier for the government to pay them back. Take, for example, a government bond sold for $1,000. After 20 years of inflation at 9%, the real value of this bond will now be only $116. Therefore, unexpected inflation can be an effective way for a government to reduce its debt to GDP ratio. However, there is a drawback: if a country gets a reputation for high inflation, people will not buy bonds unless the government offers a high interest rate. So high inflation can increase the cost of debt interest payments in the long term. But, in the 1970s and 2022, the rate of inflation was higher than expected, which did help some governments reduce their real debt to GDP ratio.

Hyperinflation in 1920s Germany.

HYPERINFLATION

In the West, an inflation rate of over 5% is often considered problematic; it causes uncertainty and discourages firms from taking on risky investment, because they are less certain of future costs and income. Even so, inflation in single digits is relatively manageable. However, sometimes inflation can rise out of control and reach astronomical figures.

For example, by October 1923, Germany was experiencing a monthly inflation rate of 29,500%, with prices doubling every 3.7 days. During this kind of inflation, money becomes rapidly useless. As soon as people receive a pay cheque, they need to spend it before prices rise and it becomes worthless. When money devalues very quickly, people lose all confidence in the economic system. Nobody wants to save in banks and people may respond by switching to a barter economy – getting paid in physical items, such as food. Also, we often see people switching to another currency that holds its value.

Hyperinflation occurs when a government prints money much faster than the growth of output in the economy. For example, in 1922, Germany faced declining output, partly due to war reparations. In response, the government began printing money to be able to pay workers. But this started a process of higher inflation. As inflation increased, workers demanded wages keep up, so there was ever-increasing pressure on the government to print more money, causing inflation to accelerate out of control. If we look at a modern example – Zimbabwe in 2008 – we find a very similar story. An economy contracting – in this case due to poor policies – and the government responding by printing money.

18
Deflation

Deflation is a period of falling prices. It means the inflation rate will be negative and the average cost of living will be decreasing.

At first glance, falling prices appears to be a good thing for households and individuals, who will be able to buy more goods for the same amount of income. However, although this may sound like a paradox, a period of deflation can often be damaging to the economy, and it is something central banks generally seek to avoid.

WHY FALLING PRICES CAN BE BAD

The big issue is: what causes deflation? Often deflation occurs due to falling demand in the economy. If the economy is weak and households are seeing a fall in real income, they will reduce spending. If firms have unsold goods and spare capacity, they may decide to cut prices to try to sell their unsold goods. With falling prices, firms will also be seeking to cut (or freeze) the wages they pay. This is the real problem of deflation: prices fall, but wages are stagnant or become lower. In this scenario, workers may not be willing to spend even though prices are lower, because they are conscious their wages are also falling. Also, if

If the price of televisions keeps falling, consumers will hold off buying them, as they expect a better price in the future.

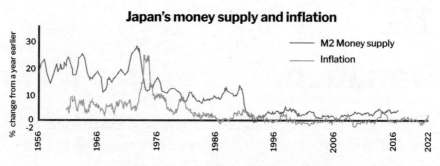

Japan suffered a long period of zero inflation or deflation.

consumers are aware that prices are falling, this can encourage them to delay big purchases. If the price of big TVs is falling 5% a year, it makes sense to wait until TVs are cheaper in the future, especially if your own finances are tight. But, if many households are thinking the same, this can cause quite a substantial fall in demand in the economy, leading to lower economic growth and rising unemployment, all of which puts more downward pressure on prices. During the 1990s and 2000s, Japan suffered a prolonged period of deflation, a phenomenon that was marked at times: consumers were reluctant to spend, hoping prices would fall further in the future.

There is another problem with deflation: it can cause the real value of debt to increase. Suppose you take out a £10,000 loan, in the hope that your wages will increase by 3% a year. However, if there is deflation and wages fall, it becomes harder to pay back this debt. Deflation increases the value of cash, but it also increases the value of debt. Therefore, in a period of deflation, households and firms who have large debts find it harder to pay it back. A greater percentage of their disposable income will have to go to servicing their debt, leaving less spending for other items. This is known as a deflationary debt spiral.

EFFECT OF DEFLATION ON SAVERS

Of course, the reverse of this is that deflation is good for savers. Falling prices mean that even if you hold cash, the value of your savings rises and will, in the future, purchase more items. However, this greater incentive to save can cause problems to the wider economy. This is something John Maynard Keynes called the paradox of thrift. For an individual to increase their savings is entirely rational, but when the majority of the population start saving more and spending less, this will cause a

John Maynard Keynes.

temporary fall in demand and lead to an economic recession with rising unemployment – hence the paradox. Therefore, thrift may make sense for an individual but will cause problems for the whole economy. This is another potential problem of deflation – an increased incentive to save leads to lower growth in the short term.

In the long term, higher savings can be beneficial, especially if an economy previously had a low savings ratio. Also, higher savings increases the potential for higher investment (because banks in receipt of more deposits are able to lend more to firms). But, if there is deflation, will we see higher investment? Probably not. The problem is that firms are concerned their revenues will fall if prices fall, so the return from investment will be limited. Also, even though banks are willing to lend, firms may be reluctant to borrow because deflation will increase the real value of debt.

Another feature of deflation is that it can complicate monetary policy and the setting of interest rates. During a recession with falling economic output, the central bank is likely to cut interest rates to stimulate demand and economic growth. However, with deflation, monetary policy becomes less effective because interest rates cannot be cut below 0%. A negative interest rate means consumers have to pay banks to hold their savings. Therefore, with deflation, the desired interest rate may not be possible and the effective real interest rate is too high for the economic situation, causing lower economic growth.

GOOD DEFLATION

The above reasons suggest why deflation can be harmful to an economy and cause a prolonged period of economic stagnation, high unemployment and low growth. However, it is possible to have a good form of deflation, where prices fall, but output increases. This deflation is caused by the rapid development of technology, which leads to lower costs of production. In this case, firms can both increase output and reduce their costs. The increased efficiency enables them to cut prices for consumers, while also

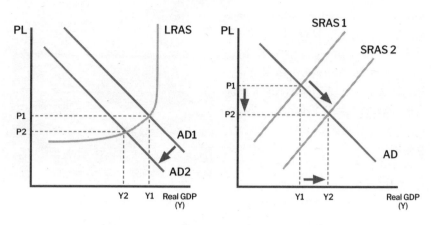

*Deflation can be caused by a fall in demand (AD)
or an increase in aggregate supply (AS).*

making bigger profits and paying higher wages. In this scenario, lower prices don't cause lower spending because households are seeing an effective rise in their real disposable income.

We have had deflation for certain items in the economy – for example, electronic goods have fallen in price in the past 50 years, and this has enabled us to purchase a greater variety of more powerful goods. If this technological improvement was spread across the entire economy, then in theory we could see lower prices and improved living standards. This is a possibility with a new technology like artificial intelligence or a new source of energy like nuclear fission. If energy became much cheaper, prices would fall, but it would be compatible with higher real incomes.

Generally speaking, it is rare for an economy to experience the 'good' form of deflation. Although prices in individual sectors of the economy may fall, it is rare for the service sector to have falling prices without falling wages. Therefore, in recent years, central banks have usually targeted an inflation rate of 2%. They would rather have a moderate rate of inflation than zero inflation and risk the problems associated with deflation.

19
Stagflation

Stagflation is a period of high unemployment and high inflation. It is an undesirable economic situation because governments and central banks face a trade-off and it is difficult (if not impossible) to tackle both issues at once.

Stagflation can be measured through what is appropriately referred to as the misery index. The misery index is simply the inflation rate + the unemployment rate. The more misery in the economy, the more stagflation is likely to be a problem.

CAUSES OF STAGFLATION
Stagflation is usually caused by a rise in the price of raw materials or other costs of production. For example, a substantial rise in oil prices will lead to a higher price of transport and living costs, causing cost-push

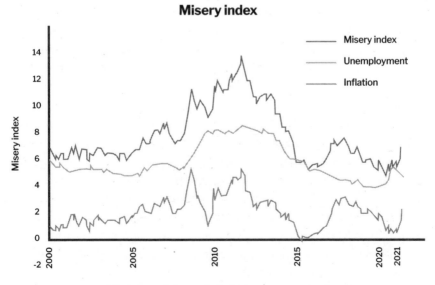

Misery index

The misery index = the inflation rate + unemployment.

Stagflation

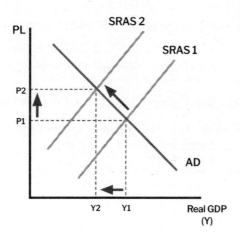

With stagflation, higher inflation occurs and there is a fall in output.

inflation (see page 81) to rise. As businesses face higher costs and push up prices, they may also have to make workers redundant because they cannot absorb all the costs. Also, as households and consumers are faced with rising prices, their effective income is reduced, causing them to cut back on spending in order to pay higher transport and energy bills. This fall in consumer spending will exacerbate the lower economic growth and cause potentially more unemployment as firms lay off workers due to the falling demand.

For example, a major period of stagflation occurred in the 1970s after the 1973–74 Oil Shock saw oil prices triple. It was a shock for firms who were forced to put up prices, but the inflation was also a shock for household budgets who saw more of their income evaporate on dealing with the higher prices. Western economies like the UK and US saw an unwelcome situation of both rising unemployment and inflation. In 2022 we saw a return of stagflation due to the energy price shock related to COVID and the conflict in Ukraine. Again we saw rising prices, but without the rising incomes. Therefore, we saw a fall in real income and lower economic growth. Unemployment often lags behind the rise in inflation, but if inflation remains high for a considerable time, firms will start to cut jobs too.

Other causes of stagflation could involve powerful trade unions. If unions can push up wages, this will cause wage-push inflation, but firms may not be able to afford the above-inflation wage increases and this could lead to less employment. Stagflation is also more likely in periods of economic decline, where a traditional industry is closing down, leading to structural unemployment. This base level of structural unemployment is unrelated to the economic cycle, so if cost-push inflation increases, the economy faces both unemployment and inflation at the same time.

PHILLIPS CURVE TRADE-OFF

The Phillips curve is a plot of inflation and unemployment rates. It suggests there can be an inverse relationship between the two. In normal economic circumstances a strong economy with a high rate of economic growth will see a period of rising employment and falling unemployment. However, as the economy approaches full capacity, this starts to cause a rise in inflation. This is the classic trade-off of falling unemployment and rising inflation.

To moderate the inflationary increases, a central bank could increase interest rates to slow down the economy. Higher interest rates will cause lower inflation but could also cause unemployment to rise as the economic cycle changes. Similarly, in a recession with high unemployment and low inflation, the central bank can reduce unemployment by cutting interest rates. This shows, at least in the short term, that the central bank faces a choice – it can choose

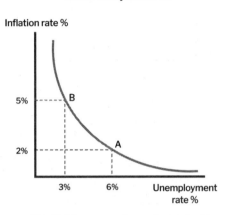

The Phillips curve

The Phillips curve shows the trade off between inflation and unemployment.

different trade-offs between inflation and unemployment. However, in a period of stagflation, this trade-off breaks down. With rising unemployment and rising inflation, the central bank cannot solve the problem with monetary policy alone.

DEALING WITH STAGFLATION

There is no magic bullet to dealing with stagflation. A central bank may decide the best thing to do is bring down inflation and suffer high unemployment in the short term. High interest rates and/or tight fiscal policy would cause lower economic growth and slowly start to squeeze inflation lower. However, if the cost-push inflation pressures are strong and inflation expectations are high, a significant economic downturn may be required in order to reduce inflation and change people's expectation of inflation. In this case, the unemployment problem will get significantly worse, which may be politically damaging for the government. In the early 1980s, both the United Kingdom and United States were experiencing stagflation and high inflation. However, the government of Mrs Thatcher was determined to break the inflationary cycle, even at the cost of a deep recession. Interest rates in the UK rose to very high levels (17%) and government borrowing reduced, causing a deep recession in which unemployment rose to 3 million. Supporters argued that this was a necessary step to end the cycle of high inflation, and in the long term the economy recovered. Critics argued that the recession was deeper than necessary, causing rates of unemployment that were both unacceptably high and unnecessary.

20
Recessions

Recessions are periods of significant decline in economic activity, usually shown by falling GDP, rising unemployment and falling investment.

They are part of the economic cycle and can be quite short-lived or become prolonged depressions.

CAUSES OF RECESSION

Recessions can be caused by a variety of factors. The most common recession is the result of a deliberate attempt of a central bank to reduce inflationary pressure in the economy. To do so, the bank will increase interest rates, reducing consumer spending and investment. If the rate rise is sufficient, this may cause a fall in overall demand, leading to a recession. Once output starts to fall, we can often see a multiplier effect causing the initial fall in demand to be magnified by rising unemployment, causing even further falls in spending. The only redeeming feature of a recession caused by this kind of demand shock is that once the central bank has recognized the economy is in recession and inflation reduced, it will cut interest rates, which should reverse the economic downturn and allow the economy to recover.

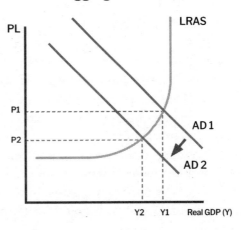

Recession caused by a fall in aggregate demand

SUPPLY SHOCK RECESSION

A very different kind of recession is caused by a supply-side shock that leads to higher prices. For example, a sharp rise in oil prices will cause a rise in costs for businesses and

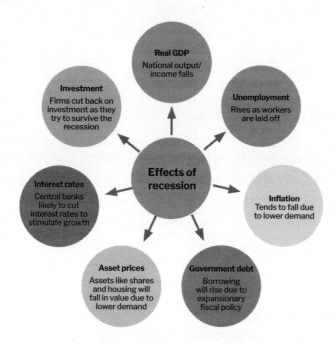

households and constrain their spending elsewhere. This can cause a recession but has the added downside of also causing inflation. Therefore, central banks have the unenviable task of trying to reduce inflation and prevent recession at the same time. They usually hope the rise in oil prices will prove temporary and short-lived. But, if prices keep rising as they did in 2022, this can be a powerful force for causing a recession.

BALANCE SHEET RECESSION

One of the most prolonged and deepest recessions of recent years was the Great Financial Crisis of 2008–09. In this case, there was no obvious demand side shock or boom and bust situation. Rather, the recession was caused by hidden problems in the banking sector. During the early 2000s the US housing market was booming, which caused a surge in mortgage lending. Banks became reckless in lending and then sold these low credit (sub-prime) mortgage bundles to banks around the world. In 2006, a modest rise in interest rates caused a rise in mortgage delinquencies because low-income borrowers couldn't afford to meet repayments. People had to sell at a loss, meaning that house prices fell and demand dried up. As house prices fell and more people failed to repay, bank losses mounted, not just in America but around the world.

Banks that had become used to borrowing money in the short term to remain liquid, suddenly found that the money markets dried up. Financial

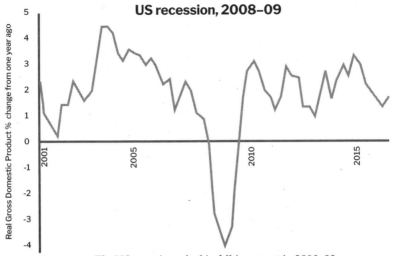

The US experienced a big fall in output in 2008–09.

institutions no longer wanted to lend to each other because they were all experiencing losses from the end of the housing bubble. As bank losses mounted, firms and households found they could no longer borrow money – even if they were very solid, with strong collateral. This lack of credit was an important factor for causing lower spending and lower investment which led to the deep recession. The recession was worsened because of the impact of falling house prices and a temporary rise in oil prices. But the main cause was the shortfall of liquidity in the banking sector. This was why this recession was quite deep and long-lasting. There was no easy fix. When central banks cut interest rates to 0%, this should have boosted demand. But, because banks didn't have any funds to lend, it didn't make much difference.

BLACK SWAN RECESSION

A final kind of recession is one called a black swan event – an unexpected and unpredictable event that causes demand side shock. For example, the COVID pandemic of 2020 led to a fall in economic activity as government lockdowns prevented people from carrying out their usual activities. This led to a very sharp fall in GDP in early 2020 when output was temporarily put on hold.

RECESSION TO DEPRESSION

There is no commonly agreed definition of a depression, but it implies a very significant fall in GDP of over 10% and/or is prolonged for two years. Harry Truman quipped: 'It's a recession when your neighbor loses his job; it's a depression when you lose yours.'

The best example is the Great Depression of the 1930s, when the initial fall in output was magnified because many medium-sized banks went bankrupt, causing more losses throughout the US economy. This led to a significant fall in the money supply and further squeezed spending and investment. Since the Great Depression, central banks have taken it upon themselves to act as lender of last resort so that ordinary commercial banks are not forced out of business, causing a loss of confidence in the banking system, which could cause a mild recession to turn into a bigger scale depression (see Moral Hazard, pages 174–7).

IMPACT OF RECESSION

A recession means that output is less than potential and indicates an underuse of resources. The most obvious cost of a recession is for those who are made unemployed, who will then experience a loss of income, fall in employability and stress-related issues caused by being out of work. If the recession is short-lived, the unemployment may prove temporary, but during disruptive recessions, whole industries may close down, and this may cause a significant degree of structural unemployment that is difficult to fix. In a recession, many firms will be forced out of business and close permanently. There is a theory that only the most inefficient firms go out of business and so recessions can actually enable the economy to revitalize. Sometimes new innovative companies are created in the depth of a recession, and these go on to be quite successful. However, firms who close down in a recession may actually be quite efficient; it was just that the recession really hit demand very hard. For example, the COVID-induced recession of 2020–21 hit hospitality firms, even the best. Without government support, many more would have gone out of business.

The coronavirus pandemic led to recession in 2020–21.

21

Unemployment

Unemployment leads to a loss of potential output but more importantly can be devastating on a personal level. A worker who is unable to find employment is left with substantially lower income plus the stress and psychological cost of not being able to do a meaningful job.

CAUSES OF UNEMPLOYMENT

There are several different causes of unemployment which have different effects on the unemployed. One type of unemployment is known as frictional unemployment, which is unemployment due to the difficulties in moving from one job to another. This is not necessarily a bad thing if the duration is short and the time period enables the worker to find a job suited to their skills. For example, if one job ends, it may take a few weeks to find a new job in a similar field. There is always a degree of frictional unemployment in any economy, and this is why economists might say that 'full employment' is actually an unemployment rate of 2–3%, because it is not possible or even desirable to eliminate this frictional unemployment completely. A graduate with a degree in engineering

Causes of unemployment

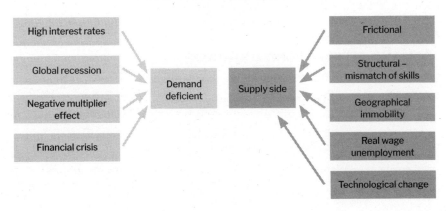

An unemployment parade in the US in 1909.

would be wasting the potential of that degree by taking the first available job, especially if the job was unskilled.

A more serious type of unemployment is known as structural unemployment, which occurs when a worker lacks the relevant skills or qualifications to take a job where there are vacancies. When a country loses competitiveness in manufacturing, its manufacturing jobs, which are often dependent on manual labour, will be lost. If a country loses competitiveness in labour-intensive industries, it may be gaining in high-tech service sectors, such as IT or computer programming. And if the labour market was perfectly flexible, an unemployed textile worker could seamlessly move into computing. However, the textile worker may have no qualifications to do a job in IT and therefore would remain unemployed even though there are unfilled vacancies. This kind of structural unemployment can be magnified when we see rapid changes in the economy and particular regions get hit harder. A good example is the Rust Belt in the American Midwest and northeastern states. In the 1960s and '70s, there were many well-paid manufacturing jobs, but as firms closed down, these regions saw a rise in unemployment, causing an outflow of capital and labour to cities on the coasts. The Rust Belt areas declined, firms not wanting to invest and unemployed workers lacking the mobility to move to another state and get a job in a different industry. Labour is not as mobile as capital because an unemployed worker may have ties to a particular area, and moving to expensive coastal cities is not always easy.

DEMAND-DEFICIENT UNEMPLOYMENT

Another cause of unemployment is due to cyclical changes in the whole economy. When the economy is growing, firms will be hiring and taking on more staff and unemployment will be falling. However, when an economy goes into a recession and output falls, firms will start laying off workers and not hire new workers. In a recession, the average unemployment rate will rise and there are simply not enough jobs on offer – no matter how qualified you are.

US unemployment, 1901–2021

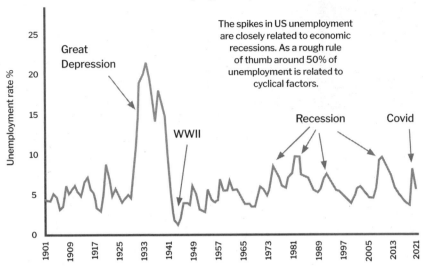

The spikes in US unemployment are closely related to economic recessions. As a rough rule of thumb around 50% of unemployment is related to cyclical factors.

Another, perhaps more controversial type of unemployment is known as real-wage or classical unemployment. This happens if trade unions can negotiate from a position of strength or minimum wages push wages significantly above the market equilibrium. As wages rise, firms demand fewer workers and this causes unemployment. The extent of real wage unemployment in modern economies is debatable. In the UK and US, trade unions are relatively weak and not able to bargain for significantly higher wages. In fact, employers have a degree of monopsony power (the power to pay lower wages in a market because there is in effect only one buyer). However, if minimum wages did rise sufficiently, this would start to cause unemployment, especially if the economy was slowing down.

REDUCING UNEMPLOYMENT

There are two main approaches to reducing unemployment – policies on the demand side or supply side. Demand-side policies include fiscal and monetary policy and are focused on reducing cyclical unemployment by stimulating economic activity. For example, in a recession the central bank can cut interest rates to encourage investment, or the government can invest in public works schemes to create demand and create employment. This was the principle behind President Roosevelt's New Deal for the United States in the early 1930s and recent fiscal stimulus packages such as in 2009, after the Global Financial Crisis.

SUPPLY-SIDE APPROACH

Supply-side economists tend to play down the role of demand management, arguing that central banks and the government often create as many problems as they solve because fiscal policy can easily cause inflation and higher borrowing and do little to solve long-term unemployment. They argue that the key to reducing unemployment is overcoming market failures and making labour markets more flexible. They may point to highly regulated European labour markets and argue that the costs of hiring and firing discourage firms from employing workers in the first place. If an employer has lower costs and less regulation, they may be more motivated to create jobs in the first place. The balancing act is that if workers have few rights they can be put onto zero-hours contracts, which creates economic insecurity and in the long term leads to lower motivation and productivity. One policy all economists tend to agree on is the desirability of improving education and training. This gives workers the flexibility to respond to a changing labour market and move from one sector to another.

Another policy to reduce unemployment could be a maximum working week. For example, France introduced a maximum working week of 35 hours. The argument is that if workers work fewer hours, a firm will have to employ more people, and this will reduce unemployment. However, the reality is not so simple. Rather than employing more workers, firms may find ways to get more out of the existing workers in those 35 hours. Some skilled labour cannot be easily replaced. For example, a manager may have done 51 hours a week before the regulation. But it doesn't make sense to employ one manager for 35 hours and then another part-time manager to do the remaining 16 hours a week. Also, more regulations may encourage firms to find ways around them. Rather than employing directly, firms may start to subcontract jobs to self-employed workers who are not subject to the maximum working week. The 35-hour working week in France was popular with many workers, but there was no strong evidence it had any real impact on reducing unemployment.

Roosevelt's New Deal in the 1930s used fiscal stimulus to create new jobs.

22
Boom and Bust

Economic growth is not always stable, and can be subject to cycles of boom and bust. An economic boom implies a period of rapid economic growth, rising asset prices and inflationary pressures.

A bust is when this period of strong growth reverses and goes into a recession, with declining economic output and rising unemployment.

An economic boom can occur for various reasons. For example, if the central bank pursues a loose monetary policy – keeping interest rates low and/or increasing the money supply – this has the effect of increasing consumer spending and improving economic growth. Low interest rates on their own may not cause a boom; there usually needs to be other factors to encourage higher demand. A very important factor in an economic boom is consumer confidence. When confidence is high, consumers are willing to borrow more and take risks with spending. This confidence will also spill over into firms. If firms see a growth in consumer spending, they will want to take on investment projects. This increase in investment will also have the effect of boosting aggregate

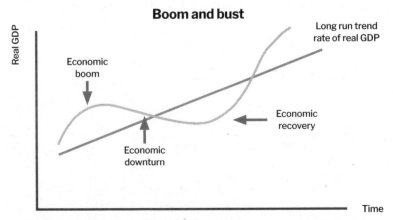

Boom and bust refers to the economic cycle of recovery and downturns.

demand, creating more employment and spending in the economy. It can lead to a multiplier effect, with a bigger final increase in output.

Another feature of economic booms is a rise in asset prices. With rising incomes, individuals will be seeking to buy assets such as housing and shares. As share prices and house prices rise, this can, in itself, encourage people to buy those same assets, to try and benefit from rising prices – an easy way to increase wealth. It is at this stage that a boom may become divorced from economic fundamentals – which means that asset prices rise above their long-term real value. People succumb to a speculative fever – sometimes known as irrational exuberance – assuming that this is an easy way to make money. Rising prices just encourage more to join.

History shows us many examples of bubbles that later burst. For example, the Railway Mania of the nineteenth century in the United Kingdom; the surge in share prices in the 1920s before the Wall Street Crash of 1929; the recent boom and bust in cryptomarkets. A good question to ask is: why do people get trapped in bubbles when so many past asset booms have ended in pain?

The answer lies in psychology. We like to think we are smarter than the market and will be able to benefit from rising prices and sell before prices decline. The second psychological element is that we tend to trust the wisdom of the crowd. If a majority of people are buying houses and shares and respected professionals are telling us it is a good time to buy, we think the majority must be right, so we jump on the bandwagon and

House price appreciation US, 1999–2017

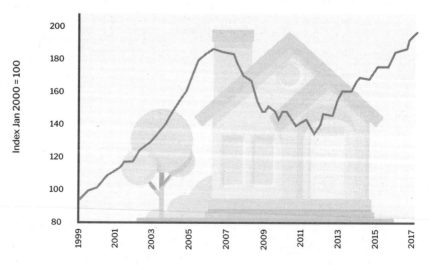

also buy. This can cause prices to rise faster than long-term averages. A good example of this was in the 2000s, when house prices rose very rapidly in the United States, Ireland and Spain. US mortgage companies were keen to cash in on booming house prices and relaxed their lending criteria to enable more to get a big mortgage. Mortgage salesmen were not thinking about long-term fair value of housing; their incentive was to sell as many mortgages as possible, even if homeowners couldn't really afford them. Banks were also willing to lend because they became caught up in the irrational exuberance that prices would keep rising. The result was a boom in house prices which increased economic growth.

However, at some point booms and bubbles come to an end. The rise in prices is unsustainable. A small rise in interest rates in 2006 caused US homeowners to struggle to pay mortgages, which led to a rise in mortgage defaults, and house prices then started to fall. Once house prices start to fall, all the factors that caused an economic boom go into reverse. Consumers lose confidence and stop spending. Banks no longer wish to lend because they are losing money, causing a decline in investment. Therefore, the economy can quite quickly go from economic boom to economic bust, with rising unemployment and recession. The biggest boom and bust was probably the late 1920s and early 1930s. Share prices became overvalued, and when they fell in 1929, this caused a loss of confidence and loss of wealth. Bad economic decisions followed, such as allowing banks to fail, and the economy declined rapidly, causing the deep recession of the 1930s.

Where possible, central banks try to avoid boom and bust economic cycles because these create a lot of instability and collateral damage. In theory, a central bank will increase interest rates if a boom is getting out of hand, and reduce growth to make it more manageable. However, this is not always easy. In the 2000s US inflation was actually quite low, and it didn't appear like there was a real economic boom. Only mortgage lending and house prices were booming, which central banks don't usually target. This is why the situation got out of hand.

Since the Global Financial Crisis, there have been few signs of economic booms as the world economy slows down. The United States had a mini boom after the end of COVID, due to generous fiscal policy, which contributed towards inflation. But this was relatively mild, caused mostly by cost-push factors.

23

Government Borrowing

When a government spends more than it receives in tax revenue, it will need to borrow the shortfall from the private sector. It does this by selling government bonds.

Bonds are typically bought by banks, pension funds and private investors, because they offer a secure investment with a guaranteed annual interest payment. Every year, the government will run either a budget deficit or (more rarely) a budget surplus. The annual deficits will add to the overall national debt, which is the total amount a government has borrowed.

REASONS FOR GOVERNMENT BORROWING

For any government there is usually a political incentive to increase borrowing in order to finance higher spending on public services and / or decrease taxation. Both higher spending and lower taxes tend to be favourable with voters. Reducing government debt tends to be less

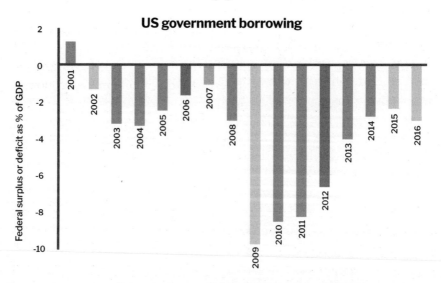

Borrowing increased during the recession of 2008–09.

politically popular. But, politics aside, there are economic reasons for government borrowing. The first is that through borrowing the government can finance public investment and spending on public goods, which are not provided by a free market. For example, investing in more public transport can increase productivity and remove bottlenecks, but this would be underprovided in a free market. Borrowing to fund investment enables higher growth in the long term, and this can improve tax revenues.

The other reason for higher government borrowing is during a recession when private sector spending falls, leading to lower output and higher unemployment. Through higher borrowing, the government can finance public spending, which helps to limit the fall in aggregate demand and enables the economy to recover more quickly from recession.

There are concerns about excess government borrowing – though economists are often more relaxed than non-economists. If government borrowing increases significantly, it may put upward pressure on interest rates because the government needs to attract more investors to buy bonds. As interest rates go up, the government will be spending more on debt interest payments rather than other areas of public spending. After the Global Financial Crisis, higher government borrowing between 2009 and 2021 did not cause rising interest rates. In fact, until 2021, interest rates fell because there was strong demand from the private sector to buy government debt. This shows that sometimes, higher government borrowing doesn't cause higher debt interest payments, which is why in periods of slow growth and low interest rates, higher government borrowing can be relatively cheap for governments.

However, there is no guarantee that rising government borrowing will always lead to low interest rates. At other points in the economic cycle, higher borrowing can be problematic. For example, in the 1970s, high inflation and high borrowing did occur with rising interest payments and the United Kingdom got into difficulties, having to borrow from the IMF. At the time of writing in 2022, interest rates are starting to rise, and this is unexpectedly causing a sharp rise in borrowing costs for European governments.

HOW MUCH CAN A GOVERNMENT BORROW?

There is no simple answer to this question. In 2022, Japanese national debt is a staggering 240% of GDP and has been high for a couple of decades, yet Japanese interest rates have been relatively low and for many years

The Greek debt crisis, 2010 protest.

there have been limited concerns over Japanese debt. This is because Japan has an ageing population with high savings and the debt is financed 90% by Japanese citizens. However, in 2008, Greece's national debt was 150% of GDP, causing a serious crisis. This was partly due to being in the eurozone and Greek debt being owned by non-Greek citizens. Worried about the ability to finance debt (and with no independent monetary policy), investors sold debt, causing Greek bond yields to surge. This led to a painful period of austerity (cutting government spending) which caused a deep recession. In Greece's case, government borrowing was unsustainably high and this, combined with the limits of being in the eurozone, led to a serious crisis. This is why the EU tries to set limits on government borrowing for members of the Euro.

In the 1950s, UK national debt rose to 240% of GDP in the aftermath of World War II; the UK was nearly bankrupt, but helped by a big loan from the US, the UK invested in public housing and set up the National Health Service. The 1950s and '60s was a period of rising prosperity and strong growth, and this continued economic growth enabled UK national debt to fall from 240% of GDP in 1950 to 38% in 1998. However, the secret here was the strong growth in the post-war period. If we are entering a period of lower growth, it is easy for debt to rise as a percentage of GDP. In the UK in 2022, with the impact of COVID-19, debt exceeded 100% of GDP for the first time since the 1960s.

IS NATIONAL DEBT LIKE A HOUSEHOLD BUDGET?

Some politicians say that a government, like a household, shouldn't live beyond its means. Revenue should equal expenditure and debt is irresponsible to future generations. The economist Paul Krugman argues this is a false analogy because the government isn't like a household. When a government borrows domestically, the country is essentially borrowing from itself. Maybe wealthy savers have excess savings sitting in bank accounts. When the government spends more and sells bonds, the wealthy savers buy bonds, which can then be put to more productive uses like investing in better education. In this case, the government is more like a household with a very rich uncle. You borrow from the uncle to be able to afford to go to university. But the net wealth of the household is unchanged; there is simply a transfer of wealth from the rich uncle to the poor student. A key factor is that if domestic savings are very high and there are unused resources, then government borrowing can

Paul Krugman.

help put it to more productive uses. However, if your household doesn't have a rich uncle, and if you don't have any savings in your family, then higher borrowing may crowd out the private sector. If the government borrows when the private sector wants to invest in private enterprise, this is a problem because the higher government spending will lead to lower private spending and probably higher interest rates.

24
Public Goods

A public good is a particular type of good or service which benefits the whole society and, once provided, is freely available for all to benefit.

In economics we say a public good has two particular characteristics – non-rivalry and non-excludability. Non-excludability means that once you provide the good, you can't stop anyone using it (even if they don't pay). For example, if you provide street lighting, the light is there for everyone. It is not like selling Netflix, where access is available only if you pay. Non-rivalry means that when you consume the good it doesn't reduce the amount available to others. If you provide 100 free apples, the amount of apples available to others reduces as they are consumed – it is not a public good. But, if there is a park and you walk around it, the park is still available to everyone else. Your consumption of the park has not affected the nature of the good.

EXAMPLES OF PUBLIC GOODS

A good example of a public good is a national park or area of outstanding natural beauty. If the government creates and looks after a national park, then everyone in the country can enjoy its beauty; you can't stop anyone visiting. To be pedantic, it may not be a pure public good – in the sense

Public libraries can be a form of a public good as they provide a service to the whole community, but they are not a pure public good, as if someone checks a book out, you have to wait for them to return it before you can read it yourself.

A police force is an example of a public good.

that if millions start to visit the national park, this may cause a degree of congestion and erosion, which means there is a degree of rivalry and excludability. But the basic principle is very close to a public good, assuming a modest number of visits. Classic examples of pure public goods can include national defence, flood defences, a justice system and street lighting. It is worth mentioning that a public good doesn't have to be just a good; it can be an attitude of always picking up litter and looking after your local community. If everyone picks up litter and keeps their streets clean, there is a benefit to everyone who lives nearby. It will also inspire others to pick up litter too.

THE FREE-RIDER PROBLEM

One important issue with public goods is that they are unlikely to be provided in a free market due to something known as the free-rider problem. This occurs when you can enjoy a good without paying for it, so there is no incentive for anyone to pay – and therefore no incentive for a firm to provide the good. For example, a rich community may be able to cooperate to provide private policing for their private estate, but for a national police force, which private firm would be willing to provide law and order for the whole country? There is no profit incentive: although the majority of citizens would benefit from law and order, it would be too difficult to make everyone pay the contribution towards it.

This is why most public goods are not left to the private market but are instead provided by the government and paid for out of general taxation. Compulsory general taxation can be seen as a way to make taxpayers contribute to the public goods that they wouldn't get in a purely free market.

Yosemite National Park: a national park is a public good, as anyone can enjoy its beauty without preventing others from enjoying it too.

Andrew Carnegie.

Not all public goods have to be left to the government. In the late nineteenth century, rich industrialists like Andrew Carnegie paid for libraries and museums across the United States. Public libraries are essentially public goods because anyone is entitled to visit, read and take out books. It is not a pure public good because sometimes you may have to wait to take a popular book, but the principle is that of a service which benefits the whole community.

NEW PUBLIC GOODS

Free Wi-Fi provision is an example of a recent service that can be seen as a public good. Internet provision is provided by the free market because internet companies can restrict access to those who have paid and get the password. However, a government or philanthropist could decide to make free internet available to everyone, free of charge. If Wi-Fi access is universally free, it becomes a public good because everyone who lives there can access without stopping others' access. Free Wi-Fi for a whole town may be more efficient than individuals buying direct. In the future, governments and local councils may see it as their duty to provide this kind of public Wi-Fi out of general taxation.

THE ENVIRONMENT

Perhaps the most important public good of all is the environment. If we look after the environment, we all benefit – not just all the people on the planet, but future generations too. If the environment is damaged, we all suffer, and if the environment is protected for future generations, we will all benefit. But, one of the reasons we do struggle to contribute to optimal environment is that it is a public good; no one individual has ownership of the water and air, and so without a collective spirit, the environment can easily be taken for granted.

PUBLIC GOODS WITHOUT A GOVERNMENT

In modern capitalistic societies, there is quite a strong free-rider aspect. We don't contribute to public goods because we tend to think in terms of personal benefits and personal costs. (At least, this is the traditional economic view of people.) However, anthropologists and sociologists suggest that in many societies the idea of contributing towards a public good is much more deeply embedded in social structures. For example, if there is a common area of natural resources, self-interested people may overgraze the shared resources (e.g. overfishing in the North Sea). However, the Nobel economist Elinor Ostrom found that people in local communities could actually be very effective in managing these shared areas because we seek the approval of our peers and know that acting in a collectivist way is essential to long-term welfare. With this kind of spirit, it is quite possible for communities to provide a range of public goods without outside government intervention.

A criticism of economics is that it assumes people are free riders, but in reality, we can have the capacity to think of wider objectives rather than just our own wants and needs. In the right environment, we can contribute towards public goods, proving that public goods can be provided without government intervention.

Elinor Ostrom.

25
Privatization

Privatization is the process of selling state-owned assets to the private sector.

The main argument in favour of privatization is that the private sector is more efficient in managing resources because they have a profit motive that is absent in the state sector. However, privatization can be controversial because of the transfer of assets from the whole nation to a smaller number of wealthy shareowners.

At the heart of privatization is an ideological argument about the best way to manage the economy. Should it be the government acting in the nation's interests – or the private sector seeking to maximize profit and efficiency?

WHY NATIONALIZATION?

In the twentieth century, many Western governments began nationalizing key public industries such as water, gas, electricity and public transport. The logic was that these industries were 'natural monopolies'. In other words, that the most efficient number of firms in the industry is one. With a national rail network, it is more efficient to have one national company – rather than competing tracks and infrastructure. A private monopoly is able to charge high prices because travellers face little competition. Furthermore, a private firm may ignore the social benefits of investing in services that help rural communities, but which are not profitable. This was the argument behind taking many important public utilities into public ownership – to make sure they were run in the public interest and not left to the vagaries of the free market.

REASONS FOR PRIVATIZATION

However, in the 1980s, governments in both the United Kingdom and United States believed that the nationalized industries were ripe for privatization. Large, state-owned industries have a tendency to become

The BT Tower in London.

inefficient and stagnant. When industries are owned by the government, they may become starved of funds for investment because there are more important political priorities, such as cutting taxes. In the private sector, managers are free to take more risky decisions and raise outside finance to develop expansion. In the state sector, firms may become unresponsive to market pressures because they answer to politicians rather than market forces. For example, when British Telecom was in state hands, the ability to make telephone calls was limited and the choice of new landlines was very restricted. After privatization, the firm had to adapt to a fast-changing market, offering more consumer choice and developing new technologies, and without political oversight it had greater freedom to do so.

The logic of privatization is that it enables efficiency gains, which can benefit consumers in the form of lower prices. To give one example, the privatization of BT saw average real charges fall between 1984 and 1999 by around 48%. This is a significant fall in prices – though not all this can be attributed to privatization. It was also due to improved technology, which saw lower telephone prices around the world. Also, other privatizations have proved much less successful in reducing prices because the newly privatized firms have been able to use their market power to increase prices and profits.

Another consequence of privatization it that it gives the government a short-term boost to finances. At the peak of privatization, the UK government raised £7 billion a year, equivalent to 3p off the basic rate of income tax. The tax coffers were boosted by privatization. But, once sold, profitable industries will share profits primarily to wealthy shareholders. For example, with rising oil prices, the formerly state-owned oil and gas companies have seen a significant rise in profits, but the average householder no longer shares in the benefits from these higher prices. However, supporters of privatization counter that the process itself often enabled loss-making, state-owned industries to transform themselves into profitable enterprises and governments now gain more revenue from corporation tax than through the previous direct ownership.

People buy British Gas shares in 1986 during its privatization.

The process of privatization varies significantly between different industries. For example, industries which face effective competition will be forced to keep prices relatively low. In the UK, privatization was often accompanied by the process of deregulation. This is where entry barriers are removed, allowing more competition in markets that used to be monopolies.

Often the main benefit of privatization has resulted from the simultaneous process of deregulation, in turn creating more competition. For example, airline deregulation in the United States during the late 1970s and '80s was very effective in reducing prices for airline travel in the country. Privatization has been much less successful in industries where deregulation and more competition could not be introduced. For example, train privatization has never really generated real competition.

Success depends very much on the nature of the industry. While the profit motive in industries like steel, electricity and telecoms is desirable, in industries such as healthcare and education it is much more controversial. Does a profit motive in healthcare improve social welfare? Some argue that the disciplines of the private sector and profit motive can lead to better healthcare services and lower prices of treatment. Others argue this is a public service where the profit motive isn't of great significance. In healthcare, privatization could lead to cost savings thanks to beneficial preventative measures that can't be measured by profit outcomes.

REGULATION OF PRIVATIZED FIRMS
Another key factor behind the success of privatization is the extent to which the newly privatized industry is regulated. If you create a private

monopoly, it will need regulating on issues such as price setting and setting standards of public service. The problem with regulation is that it is only a limited form of privatization because you swap complete government control for a limited form of government intervention. The key determinant of privatization is the quality of regulatory bodies. Regulators can be subject to regulatory capture, where they become too friendly to the companies they are regulating, allowing prices to rise and an increase in profits. On the other hand, firms complain that regulators can be too strict, not allowing sufficient price rises to enable long-term investment in the industry.

There is no immediate metric for determining the success of privatization. Numerous examples provide only conflicting reports about the ability to reduce prices, increase productivity and increase profits. But it does highlight an important ideological divide between those who argue the economy is best left to the free market and those who prefer industries to be run in the public interest.

	Privatization	Nationalization
Ownership	Firm owned by private sector	Firm owned and managed by government
Incentives	Profit motive acts as incentive for owners and managers	Workers may feel motivated if they feel company belongs to them
Externalities	Private firm may ignore external costs (e.g. pollution) and external benefits	Government can put social benefits above profit motive
Efficiency	Incentive to introduce new technologies and increase labour productivity	Nationalized firms may find it hard to sack surplus workers
Knowledge	Private firms employ managers with the best skills	Politicians may interfere based on political motives
Natural monopolies	Private monopolies may charge high prices	Government can set prices based on social factors

26
Bond Markets

In 2021, the global bond market was estimated to be around $119 trillion. A bond is a form of debt issued to those willing to buy the bond in return for an annual interest payment.

The largest form of bonds are government bonds, used to finance public sector debt. In addition, there are bond markets for companies (corporation bonds) and mortgage-related debt. The bond market includes both a primary market, where individuals can buy bonds directly from those issuing them, and also the secondary market, where bonds can be bought and sold before the bond matures.

BOND PRICES AND INTEREST RATE
A typical government bond could be issued for $1,000 at an annual interest rate of 5% for 30 years. This means a buyer of a bond would get paid $50 a year for the next 30 years. At the end of the bond term, they would receive the full capital amount of $1,000. For the government, selling bonds is a way to spend more than they receive in taxation. For

A US government bond from 1981.

individuals and pension funds who buy bonds, the advantage is that they get both an annual interest payment and a secure form of saving money.

The secondary market is where these bonds can be traded between buyers and sellers. The price of bonds and the effective interest rate (known as yield) fluctuate in an inverse relationship. Suppose that there is great demand for buying bonds because they are seen as an attractive option. In this case, higher demand for bonds will lead to an increase in the market price to say $1,200. However, as the bond price increases, the effective yield on the bond will go down. Investors will still be entitled to $50 a year (5% of initial sum). But as a percentage of $1,200, the yield has fallen to 4.16%. If the bond rose in price to $2,000, the yield would fall further, to 2.5%.

Similarly, if investors expected interest rates to rise, the bonds with a 5% yield would be less attractive because they could get better rates of return elsewhere. In this case, the price of these bonds would fall as people sell. As the bond price falls, the effective yield on the bond would rise. If the price fell to $500, the effective yield would rise to 10%.

This is why as bond prices rise, yields fall. Conversely when bond prices fall, yields rise.

BOND YIELD CURVE

There are different types of bonds available to buy. These can include short-term bonds (e.g. three months or a year) and long-term bonds (e.g. 30 years). The importance of this is that the yield on long-term bonds can give an indication of what the market expects to happen to inflation in the future. If markets expect persistently high inflation in the future, this reduces the value of money, so investors require a higher bond yield on long-term bonds to compensate for the effect of future inflation. However, if markets expect deflation, the value of money increases and the yield on long-term bonds will be lower as a result. An inverted yield curve is said to occur when the yield on long-term bonds is less than short-term bonds, and this is said to indicate that the markets predict low growth and deflation over time. Bond markets have correctly predicted a worsening economic situation several times, although they are not foolproof and investors can get it wrong.

GOVERNMENT BONDS

The most important bond market is that of government (sovereign debt). For an advanced economy like the US, UK or Germany, government bonds are viewed as a very secure investment because these governments have never defaulted. However, economies with a history of debt default are likely to need higher bond yields to attract sufficient investors. Argentina has defaulted on its debt five times since 1824, so there is a premium on Argentina bond yields to compensate for the higher risk of bond holders losing out to inflation or government default. In 2022, yields on Argentinian bonds reached 49%, compared to 0.2% in Japan and 4% in the UK.

There is a greater risk of debt default if a country finances bond sales by selling to overseas investors. In the early 1980s, many poor countries attracted capital flows from rich countries, which enabled them to borrow more and sell bonds. However, when the capital flows dried up and the Western banks wished to be reimbursed, the developing economies couldn't meet the debt interest and debt repayments, leading to default and the rise in Third World debt.

An interesting example of the bond market was in 2012, when several countries in the eurozone saw problems in their bond market and rising bond yields. Countries including Greece, Ireland and Italy saw a rise in budget deficits during the 2009–10 recession. This raised the possibility that they would have difficulty meeting their debt repayments, so markets began to steer clear of these country's bond markets. If demand falls, bond yields rise, indicating stress in the bond market. The problem is

EU bond yields

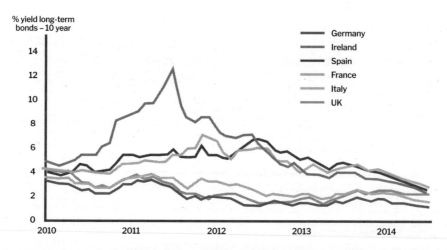

Some European countries had a spike in bond yields in 2012–13.

that countries within the eurozone did not have their own currency, so the central bank of each country could not solve the liquidity problem by printing more money and reassuring markets.

In the UK (which actually had a higher budget deficit), bond yields stayed very low. The difference was that the UK is outside the eurozone, which means that it retained independence of monetary policy and could increase the money supply to buy bonds. This is why a country with its own currency can always avoid default by printing money. The only drawback is that printing too much money will cause inflation, reducing the value of bonds indirectly. Inflation reduces the value of a bond. If an investor buys a 5% bond expecting inflation of 2%, they can make a real return of 3%. But, if inflation ends up being 9% and the yield is only 5%, this is in effect a real decline of 4%. Therefore, inflation can cause a partial default and make investors wary about buying bonds in the future.

27
Exchange Rates

Exchange rates measure the value of one currency against another.

For example, in March 2022, £1 was worth $1.31. Back in 1900, £1 GBP would have got you $4.50. This indicates that over the past 100 years, the US economy has outperformed the UK economy, making the dollar worth relatively more, and more attractive as a source of investment.

DETERMINING EXCHANGE RATES

The value of a currency is determined in a similar way to every other good – basic supply and demand. If the US dollar becomes in greater demand, it will appreciate (rise) in value against other currencies. This demand for currencies will be determined by several factors. In the long term, an important factor is relative inflation rates. Suppose inflation in Japan is 0% and in India 5%; this means that the price of Indian goods is increasing at a faster rate than Japanese. As Indian goods become more expensive, consumers will import relatively fewer Indian goods and more Japanese goods. This will cause an increase in demand for the Yen and lower demand for the Indian Rupee. In other words, the Yen will appreciate against the Rupee.

Exchange rates between currencies are determined by supply and demand.

In the short term, the value of the exchange rate can be influenced by interest rates. Suppose the Reserve Bank of India, the country's central bank, were concerned about the fall in the value of the Rupee. It could increase interest rates to make it more attractive to save in Indian banks. If interest rates in India are raised to 10% and in Japan they are only 0%, financial institutions now have a strong incentive to deposit money in Indian banks to benefit from high interest rates. For pension funds with billions of dollars to invest, even a small change in interest rates may make it worthwhile moving funds from one country to another.

However, it is not only interest rates that are important. Even high interest rates may not be sufficient if investors don't have confidence in an economy. For example, in September 2022, Argentina increased interest rates to 75% – a very high return – but investors are still put off by the very high inflation and history of government default. Another thing to bear in mind is that investors are always trying to beat the market. Investors will not wait for interest rates to rise. If you think there is a chance US interest rates will rise in the future, you will buy dollars in anticipation – hoping to make profit from a later rise in the dollar. Therefore, day-to-day movements in exchange rates may not always seem logical but can be determined by expectations for economic growth, political stability, inflation and interest rates.

THE IMPACT OF A FALLING EXCHANGE RATE

If there is a fall in the exchange rate (termed depreciation or devaluation), this will have both positive and negative effects for an economy. Generally, consumers will lose out because the price of imported goods will rise, but exporters will see an increase in competitiveness. Suppose the exchange rate is £1 = €1.30. Buying a €13,000 car from Europe will cost a UK citizen £10,000. However, if Pound Sterling falls in value to say £1 = €1.00, buying the same €13,000 car will now cost £13,000. Even though the car has not changed price in Euros, importing the car is now 30% more expensive for UK consumers.

A significant devaluation can contribute to cost-push inflation, especially for economies that import a high percentage of food, goods and raw materials. It is also the type of inflation that can make people worse off. If the exchange rate falls 30% in value, and there is no change in your salary, the purchasing power of your currency falls significantly.

On the positive side, exporters will now find their goods are more attractive. Suppose a UK firm was selling a bicycle for £5,000. This used

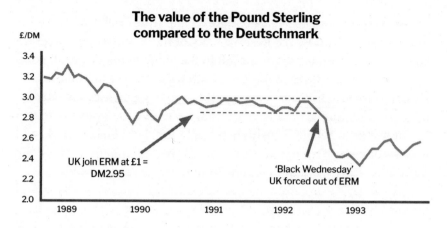

The value of the Pound Sterling compared to the Deutschmark

to cost European customers €6,500. But, after the fall in the value of the Pound, Europeans can now buy the bicycle for €5,000. This should lead to an increase in export demand, higher economic growth and an improvement in the trade balance.

A good question is whether a depreciation in the exchange rate will help the economy or not. There is no easy answer. In the Great Depression, many economies faced negative growth, high unemployment and deflation. In this situation, countries that devalued their exchange rate saw a boost to economic growth, higher exports and only a modest effect on inflation. Therefore, in an economic downturn and an overvalued exchange rate, a depreciation can help the economy recover and unemployment to fall.

However, if inflation was already a problem and there was a rapid depreciation, this could cause inflation to increase to a problematic level. Living standards would fall and consumers would be worse off. Countries which see high inflation and a prolonged depreciation in the exchange rate will tend to have slower rates of economic growth in the long term. For example, developing economies, such as Argentina, Russia and Brazil, have all experienced negative effects from a sustained period of depreciation in their currency.

FLOATING VS FIXED EXCHANGE RATES

Countries, like the UK, US and Japan, generally do not target a particular exchange rate. They pursue what is known as a floating exchange rate. The value of a currency is determined by market forces. In the early 1990s, the UK joined the exchange rate mechanism – a precursor to the Euro. The aim was to keep the value of the Pound fixed against the Deutschmark, but UK inflation was high and market forces wanted to sell the Pound. The government tried to maintain the value of the Pound by selling foreign exchange reserves to buy Pounds and keeping interest rates very high. But this policy was ineffective. High interest rates caused a deep recession and the country started to run out of foreign currency reserves. In 1992, the UK government was forced to leave the ERM and devalue the Pound.

China, by contrast, has been more successful in unofficially targeting its exchange rate. China has a large trade surplus due to a successful export industry. Normally, this would lead to an appreciation in the Yuan – but this would make Chinese exports less competitive. To keep the currency undervalued, the Chinese state banks have eagerly bought foreign assets (selling Yuan to buy foreign assets and currency). China has also used capital controls to limit the amount of currency that can be taken out of the country. The Chinese currency is increasingly important because of the size of the Chinese economy.

28
Balance of Payments

The balance of payments records international flows between one country and the rest of the world. It includes both government and private sector transactions.

The balance of payments is composed of two main parts – the current account and the capital account (also classified as the financial account). The current account receives most interest because it records net flows of goods and services. A current account deficit means that the country is importing more goods and services than it exports.

If a country runs a current account deficit, then in a floating exchange rate, it must run a surplus on the financial/capital account (see Exchange Rates, pages 122–5). The two components have to balance because a country wanting to finance net imports needs the foreign exchange to pay for it.

EXPLAINING WHY THE BALANCE OF PAYMENTS MUST BALANCE

Suppose the United States runs a current account deficit with China because it is a net importer of manufactured goods. This means China will be receiving substantial foreign exchange payments in return for exporting goods. Gaining foreign exchange, China will want to do something with this surplus foreign exchange, so it may buy US government bonds or invest in US assets. Therefore, the United States pays say $100 billion to buy imports. But, China ends up spending $100 billion to buy US financial and physical assets. If China stopped buying US foreign exchange assets, what would happen? The dollar would devalue because more dollars were being supplied than demanded. As the dollar depreciated, US goods would become relatively cheaper and Chinese imports relatively more expensive. The dollar would fall until the US current account deficit with China was wiped out. This is why China has often been happy to buy US assets. It gains financial clout

Balance of payments equilibrium

A deficit on the current account
is balanced by a surplus on the
financial account

Financial account
· Direct investment (FDI)
· Portfolio investment
(bonds, saving, equities)

+ $100 billion
(surplus)

Current account
· Trade in goods
· Trade in services
· Investment incomes
· Transfer payments

- $100 billion
(deficit)

This country is using capital
inflows to finance consumption
of imports and investment

with the United States, but importantly helps to keep Chinese exports competitive, a big source of economic growth.

IS IT A PROBLEM TO RUN A CURRENT ACCOUNT DEFICIT?

Often it is assumed that a current account deficit is a bad sign or harmful to the economy. It suggests the country is lacking in competitiveness and living beyond its means – relying on foreign imports. Also, a current account deficit means that foreigners will have an increasing claim on

The Asian Financial Crisis of 1997.

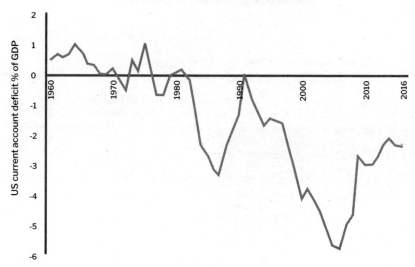

*The current account deficit refers to the value of
imports of goods and services greater than exports.*

domestic assets. For example, the UK has run a current account deficit since the mid-1980s. It has financed this deficit by attracting capital inflows, e.g. foreigners buying up property and firms in the UK. Another significant problem with a large current account deficit is that it may be vulnerable to a depreciation in the currency. If a country has a deficit, but then capital flows dry up, the exchange rate will fall, causing a loss of confidence and higher import prices. This is particularly an issue for emerging economies who can more easily be subject to capital flight. If investors lose confidence, the exchange rate will fall. Balance of payments issues was a factor behind the Asian Financial Crisis of 1997, where countries saw capital flight and depreciations of over 25%.

DON'T PANIC ABOUT THE DEFICIT

However, in many cases, countries can run prolonged current account deficits without any ill effects, and actually this enables households to have a better standard of living because they are able to consume more goods. After sanctions were imposed on Russia in early 2022, the country's current account balance of payments improved. The reason is that it was still exporting gas and oil (at high prices) but sanctions severely limited the ability to import consumer goods. It even led to a relatively strong Rouble because Russians were not selling Roubles to buy foreign goods. However, although there was a big surplus in the current account, a fall in living standards did follow because the availability of goods was significantly reduced. It shows you can't measure the success of an economy by the current account. In reverse, the fact that the United States has often run a current account deficit means household consumption is greater than if it relied on domestic production and the trade deficit had to balance.

Also, capital flows which help finance a current account deficit can also be beneficial to the domestic economy. For example, foreign capital flows can help build new factories and energy sources, which help the economy to grow. The US has often run a current account deficit, and has benefitted from capital flows with foreigners buying US debt and US securities. This means US debt is partially funded by foreign capital inflows – making it cheaper for the US government to borrow money. On the other hand, capital flows may not always benefit an economy. If an emerging country borrows to finance imports, this is likely to be unsustainable and cause higher debt problems in the future. This was a key factor behind the Third World debt crisis which exploded in the 1980s. Developing economies borrowed to run a current account deficit – enabling the greater import of goods and components, but when interest rates rose, they ended up owing large sums of debt repayments.

HOW TO REDUCE A CURRENT ACCOUNT DEFICIT

Suppose a government was concerned about the size of a current account deficit – what could it do to reduce the deficit? The easiest way to reduce the deficit would be to pursue policies that reduced consumer spending, such as higher taxes and/or lower government spending. This would reduce aggregate demand and therefore spending on imports. Also, it would have the added benefit of reducing inflationary pressures and making domestic goods relatively more attractive. However, the very obvious disadvantage is that it would lead to lower economic growth and

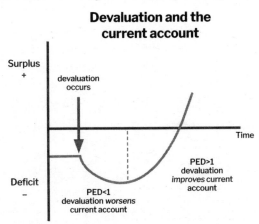

Devaluation and the current account

higher unemployment (and therefore be unpopular!). An alternative policy would be to devalue the exchange rate. If there is a fall in the value of the exchange rate, then the current account is likely to improve. This is because exports become relatively cheaper and imports more expensive. Assuming demand is relatively elastic (responsive to price changes), the value of exports will increase and the value of imports decrease.

The problem of depreciation is that it will reduce living standards because imported goods will be more expensive. It can also increase inflationary pressures because imports will go up. Higher inflation will in turn reduce competitiveness and therefore, the current account may not actually improve in the long term. The only really sustainable way to improve the current account is to improve general productivity and competitiveness. For example, supply-side reforms which increase labour productivity will enable exporting firms to be more competitive. Investing in public infrastructure such as better transport may also reduce costs. If successful, this will help boost exports without any side effects, but in the real world it is difficult to achieve this increased competitiveness through government policy alone. Most productivity growth comes from private sector innovation.

29

Monetary Policy

Monetary policy involves attempts to control the supply and demand of money in order to target inflation and economic growth.

Monetary policy used to be operated by governments, but over the years more countries have given control to independent central banks. The rationale is that independent economists are less swayed by political pressures and will avoid the temptation to cut interest rates before an election. The main tool of monetary policy is interest rates, because these have a very significant impact on economic activity.

The central bank does not directly set the interest rate that your bank offers you. It sets a key interest rate called the base rate or repo rate. Basically, this is the interest rate that commercial banks pay for borrowing from the central bank. If this base rate changes, commercial banks will usually (though not always) pass this change on to the consumer. The primary target of monetary policy is to keep inflation low. For example, in the eurozone the European Central Bank (ECB) has an inflation target of less than 2%. But, in addition to inflation, central banks will usually consider the effect on economic growth and unemployment.

REDUCING INFLATION

Suppose an economy was overheating, causing a rise in wages and prices, leading to inflation. In this scenario, the central bank will increase interest rates in order to 'cool down' the economy. Higher interest rates will have various effects. Firstly, it is more expensive to borrow, so consumers will think twice about putting purchases on a credit card or taking out a loan to buy a new car. Any household without a fixed mortgage rate will then see higher interest payments on their mortgage and so will have to cut back their spending to pay the mortgage. Firms will also face higher borrowing costs and so will delay investment decisions until borrowing is cheaper. Secondly, higher interest rates make it relatively more attractive

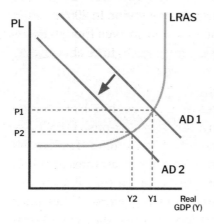

Reducing inflation through monetary policy

Higher interest rates reduce aggregate demand (AD) and inflation (PL).

to save, discouraging both spending and investment. Thirdly, higher interest rates will tend to cause an appreciation in the exchange rate. Higher interest rates in the United States will make it more attractive to deposit in US banks, so the dollar will appreciate. This appreciation will also help reduce inflation because imports are cheaper, and there will be lower export demand, leading to lower economic growth.

As growth slows, the economy will face less inflationary pressures. Equally, in a recession, cutting interest rates should boost demand, increase growth and help reduce unemployment. In theory, it seems that monetary policy could be used to fine-tune the economy and avoid both high inflation and high unemployment. And indeed sometimes this can occur. For example, the period in the United States from the late 1980s to 2007 is known as the Great Moderation because inflation was low and economic growth positive.

DIFFICULTIES OF MONETARY POLICY

However, in practice, it can be much more difficult to manage the economic cycle. Firstly, there is a time delay: if you cut interest rates, it may take a long time for householders on a fixed rate mortgage to notice. Ideally, a central bank would be able to forecast future inflation trends and change interest rates in anticipation, but it can be difficult to predict the economy accurately because there are so many variables. It can even be difficult to know where the economy is right now.

For example, the Great Recession in the United States (US) started in the first quarter of 2008, but the recession wasn't officially announced until 12 months later. The delay in knowing how serious the recession was meant monetary policy was delayed in its response.

Another problem with monetary policy is that people don't always behave like economics textbooks expect. If confidence is very low, cutting interest rates may have no effect in encouraging spending. In 2009, interest rates were cut from 5% to 0.5%, but there was little increase in spending and investment because banks, firms and consumers were all nervous about the state of the economy and the banking sector. In 2009 another problem was that banks were short of cash, and so even though it was cheap to borrow, they didn't have the liquidity (cash) to be able to lend.

DIFFICULT CHOICES

More pressing are the unexpected events that make the job of a central banker quite difficult. For example, in a period of cost-push inflation or stagflation, central bankers face an unresolvable dilemma. If inflation is high and unemployment high, do they increase interest rates to reduce inflation (and make unemployment worse), or do they cut interest rates to reduce unemployment (and make inflation worse)? They must choose one or the other – in the short term at least, they can't target both. For example, in 2022, the United States faced high inflation, but initially the Federal Reserve was reluctant to raise interest rates in case this caused a recession. It was then criticized for being too slow to act on inflation. By the end of the year, it realized that inflation was more stubborn than first thought and started raising rates quickly. This led others to criticize the Fed for risking a recession.

QUANTITATIVE EASING

The interest rate is not the only form of monetary policy that can be used. In 2009, it was cut to 0.5%, but the economy was still depressed. The central bank resorted to more unorthodox means and used something called quantitative easing (QE). This involves creating money – similar to printing money, but achieved electronically in the central bank account. The central bank then bought assets (e.g. government bonds) from banks.

This reduced the interest rates on bonds and increased the liquidity (cash reserves) of commercial banks. In theory, commercial banks with more liquidity (cash) can lend out more to business and help economic growth. The commercial banks did indeed do well out of

The European Central Bank.

this increase in the monetary base – but only a small fraction of it was used for financing investment in the real world because the banks were still reluctant to lend. QE didn't cause inflation as some had feared, but it didn't return the economy to normal growth. A related policy, which might have been more effective, is something known as a helicopter drop – where the central bank prints money and gives it directly to ordinary citizens (like dropping cash from a helicopter, but in a more controlled way). In theory, this cash leads to higher spending and higher growth more effectively than giving to commercial banks.

In many cases, though, governments printing money can lead to disaster. There are many examples where printing money caused excess inflation and destabilized economic activity. For example, the Confederacy during the American Civil War (1860–65), Germany 1922–23, Hungary 1946 and Zimbabwe 2008. Printing money causes inflation because if the amount of goods stays the same but there is more cash in circulation, firms just put up their prices. Printing money does nothing to increase actual output or wealth. Therefore, too much money will just cause inflation.

There are only certain cases where you can print money without causing inflationary problems – when an economy is seriously depressed, the interest rate is at zero, and inflation is very low or there is even deflation (falling prices). This scenario is sometimes known as a liquidity trap, but the policy of printing money in response is very rarely used, perhaps because of the fear it could lead to inflation.

Zimbabwe dollar notes from 2008, ranging from 10 dollars to 100 billion dollars.

30
Liquidity Trap

A liquidity trap is a particular set of circumstances characterized by low interest rates and low growth.

In particular, it is a situation where reducing interest rates is ineffective because individuals want to hold onto their cash savings and cannot be induced to borrow or to invest. As previously mentioned (see page 132), cutting interest rates usually increases the incentive to spend and borrow. The yield from bonds reduces as rates fall, so reducing interest rates can encourage people to sell those bonds and increase spending. However, when interest rates are close to zero, there is no cost to holding wealth in cash and so central bank activity usually has no effect in encouraging spending and investment. In this case, monetary policy is said to be like 'pushing on a piece of string' – that is, it has no effect.

WHY MIGHT WE END UP IN A LIQUIDITY TRAP?
Firstly, it could be due to very low confidence about the future state of the economy. If confidence is high, businesses will be keen to invest, but if they don't expect future demand to grow, they may as well keep their cash reserves rather than invest. In the Global Financial Crisis (GFC) of 2007–08, the low confidence in the economy was magnified because of the perilous

Japan suffered from a liquidity trap in the 1990s and 2000s.

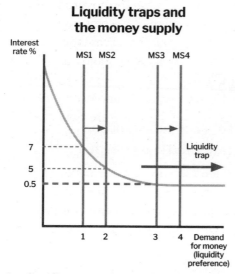

Liquidity traps and the money supply

In a liquidity trap, an increase in money supply (MS) does not cause lower interest rates.

financial state of many banks. Having lost money due to the housing bubble and bust, many banks were nursing balance sheets with large losses and were now seeking to attract more deposits, making them less willing to lend. Firms who had lost money were also seeking to improve their balance sheets rather than invest.

Secondly, in a period of very low inflation or deflation, there is greater reward to holding cash, since it does not lose its value. During the 1990s and 2000s, Japan had a prolonged period of deflation – a classic example of a liquidity trap. With deflation of 2% (prices falling 2% a year), holding cash gives you a real interest rate of +2% (the value of money increases during deflation). The real interest rate is the nominal interest rate minus inflation. In this case the interest rate was 0% and inflation -2%. Therefore, the effective real interest rate (minus -2% = +2%) is actually quite high. Even just by holding onto your cash, you will see a growth of 2% in real terms every year. In Japan, during this deflationary period, the interest rate was cut to zero, which had no effect on boosting economic growth and little on reducing deflationary pressure.

Liquidity traps may also be more likely due to certain demographic changes. When there is a young, growing population, there tends to be higher investment spending and higher growth. But, in an ageing population, there is less need for business investment and a higher preference for cash savings; this makes a liquidity trap become more probable.

SOLUTIONS TO A LIQUIDITY TRAP – FISCAL POLICY

In a liquidity trap, the Keynesian approach is to use fiscal policy because this directly leads to higher business investment and doesn't rely on the private sector responding to weak monetary signals. Fiscal policy involves changing government spending and taxation decisions. For example, if the private sector is reluctant to invest, the government can push ahead with policies to directly increase public sector investment, such as by building roads, schools or hospitals. The advantage of this is that it will directly increase overall demand in the economy and could lead to a multiplier effect, where higher public investment gives the private sector confidence and encourages it to start spending more too. Another advantage of fiscal policy is that because interest rates are close to zero, the government will be able to borrow the money at a very low interest rate, so the cost of servicing debt payments will be quite cheap. Public sector projects will need only a limited return to give a net benefit. It is true that over time, interest rates may rise and so government borrowing may become more expensive. But fiscal policy could play a bridging role in providing a short-term stimulus, with low borrowing costs while the liquidity trap remains.

Some fear fiscal policy could cause crowding out – when higher public spending causes an equivalent fall in private sector spending, meaning that there is no overall increase in demand and growth. But, in a liquidity trap this will not occur because the private sector is sitting on unused cash savings and has large cash reserves that it can lend to the government – without reducing the amount of private sector investment. In fact, fiscal policy could cause crowding in – when government fiscal stimulus causes the private sector to be more willing to spend their unused savings.

UNCONVENTIONAL MONETARY POLICY

Another approach to a liquidity trap is to use unconventional monetary policy, such as targeting higher inflation and/or increasing the money supply. For example, suppose the central bank increases the money supply by printing more money. Unless all this extra money is saved, some will lead to higher demand, which will start to cause some inflation and more normal economic activity. The key thing is that if people start

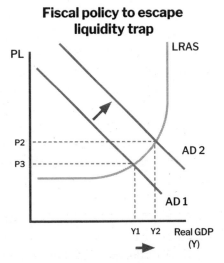

Fiscal policy to escape liquidity trap

Fiscal policy seeks to increase demand in a recession.

137

to expect higher inflation in the future it will help break the cycle of the liquidity trap. The difficulty with unconventional monetary policy is that as Paul Krugman observed, a central bank needs to 'credibly promise to be irresponsible', and this doesn't come easy to central bankers who don't want to lose their reputation for being sober, responsible and determined to keep inflation low. For two decades, the Bank of Japan has been hesitant in its attempts to break through a cycle of deflation and has never really been successful.

31
Multiplier Effect

The multiplier effect explains how an initial increase in investment can cause a bigger final increase in national output.

Suppose an economy is depressed and a government decides to spend an extra £5 billion on building 100 new hospitals. This increase in government spending will lead to an increase in national output of £5 billion. The spending leads to the purchase of raw materials, paying various suppliers and paying more wages. If all the £5 billion gets spent, it will be equivalent to increasing Gross Domestic Product (GDP) by £5 billion. But the multiplier effect notes that the increase in output may not stop there. If the unemployed gain employment in building the hospitals, they will gain income and therefore increase their spending. As a result, income for shopkeepers and online retailers will rise. This increase in demand leads to a rise in output, meaning that these unrelated businesses may have to employ more workers, which would see further increases in income. In other words, there are knock-on effects. From the initial boost,

The multiplier effect

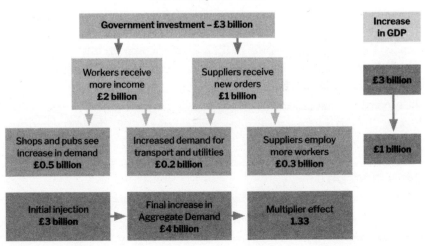

The multiplier effect

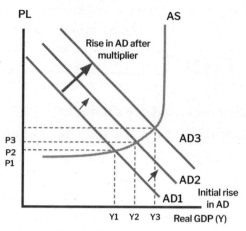

The multiplier effect relates to how an initial increase in demand may cause a bigger final rise in demand.

output continues to grow, a little bit like a snowball effect.

The injection into the economy doesn't have to come from government spending; it could come from private investment or increased export demand. For a big sporting occasion, a sudden influx of tourists may increase spending by £1 billion, and as hoteliers and restaurants receive this extra income, these businesses and their workers will also increase their spending in the economy.

LIMITS ON THE MULTIPLIER EFFECT

In theory, if a high percentage of this injection of spending into the economy leads to knock-on spending, the multiplier effect could be quite large because there are numerous rounds of extra spending. However, in the real world the multiplier effect is limited by several factors and, in some cases, may be non-existent.

The first factor that will determine the size of the multiplier effect is the amount of withdrawals from economic activity. If the workers employed to build a hospital gain extra income, they will immediately be paying more tax – so not all of that money will go back into the economy. Also, they may decide to save a certain percentage and not increase spending. Finally, they may spend some of their extra income on import spending, which doesn't increase domestic incomes (though it will increase demand in foreign countries). Therefore for every £1,000 increase in income from the government decision, the extra spending in the economy may amount to only £200, so the final multiplier effect would be 1.2. The initial injection is £1,000, and final increase in GDP is £1,200.

CROWDING OUT

But there is another major limitation of the multiplier effect. Suppose the economy is close to full employment with very low unemployment rates. If the government increase spending on new hospitals by £5 billion –

where is this extra spending going to come from? It could be higher taxes, which will reduce the disposable income of taxpayers. Alternatively, it could fund the higher spending by government borrowing, which will involve selling bonds to the private sector. After buying government bonds, the private sector has less funds for private investment. In this scenario the extra spending doesn't actually increase income by £5 billion. It merely shifts it from the private sector to the government sector. And some may argue that government spending is more inefficient than the private sector, which might even reduce economic output.

Alternatively, if the economy is close to full capacity, an increase in injections may just cause inflation. The inflow of money into the economy creates higher spending, but since firms cannot meet the higher demand, they respond by putting up prices. Real output is unaffected and so the multiplier effect is close to zero.

WHY IS THE MULTIPLIER EFFECT IMPORTANT?

The multiplier effect is important in a recession, when the government wishes to use fiscal policy to increase economic growth. If there is a positive multiplier effect, increasing government spending will be effective in reaching this goal. But, if there is no multiplier effect, fiscal policy will be of no value. This is why governments usually pursue fiscal policy when there is spare capacity and unemployed resources. In this circumstance, the multiplier effect is likely to be more effective.

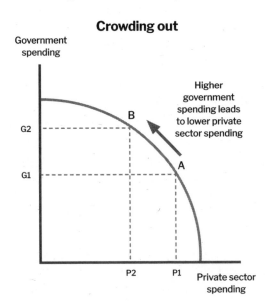

Crowding out

Government spending

Higher government spending leads to lower private sector spending

B

G2

A

G1

P2   P1   Private sector spending

NEGATIVE MULTIPLIER EFFECT

The multiplier effect can also work in reverse. If a big car firm closes down, many workers will lose their jobs, causing a fall in national income. But, if people lose their jobs, there will be less spending and businesses related to the car industry will also see lower incomes. This can be a particular problem for certain regions dependent on a key industry. When a key industry closes down, it affects the whole region because everyone is to some extent dependent on the industry. For example, the Rust Belt in the American Midwest and northeastern states is so called because the closure of big manufacturing firms caused many unemployed workers to leave and find work elsewhere, meaning the whole area declined and became poorer.

32
Comparative Advantage

Comparative advantage is a situation where a country can produce a good relatively more cheaply than another country.

The key phrase is 'relatively'. For example, an advanced industrial economy such as Germany may be able to produce a variety of goods, from food to cars, more cheaply than an emerging economy such as Argentina. However, that doesn't mean it is desirable for Germany to produce all these goods. It would be a waste of Germany's industrial potential to sacrifice skilled workers and resources to grow food. Germany and Argentina can both gain if they specialize in their areas of comparative advantage and then trade their surplus with each other.

Suppose that with a certain amount of resources Germany could produce either 1 unit of food or 4 units of cars. In this case, we can say the opportunity cost of producing that unit of food is to forego 4 units of cars. The opportunity cost is 4.

In the case of Argentina, they may have a ratio of 2 units of food to 3 cars. In this case, the opportunity cost of producing a unit of food is 3/2 (1.5).

Output per worker in one year

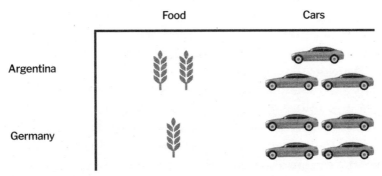

Germany has comparative advantage in producing cars.

David Ricardo developed the theory of comparative advantage.

Therefore, if Argentina specializes in producing food, it has a much lower opportunity cost. It foregoes only 1.5 units of manufacturing compared to Germany's 4 units. Specialization in their respective areas of comparative advantage enables both countries to double their output. Germany will produce 8 units of cars, and Argentina 4 units of food. The total output is greater from specialization than if they both tried to produce both food and cars.

Furthermore, the benefits of comparative advantage do not stop there. The earlier example assumes constant returns to scale, but in the real world, specializing in a particular industry is likely to cause economies of scale. As Germany specializes in manufacturing, it can get lower average costs by increasing efficiency. Argentina can gain economies of scale in agriculture.

The theory of comparative advantage was developed by nineteenth-century economist David Ricardo, who used the example of two countries, Portugal and the United Kingdom, trading wine (comparative advantage in Portugal) and cloth (comparative advantage in the UK). His theory became an important theoretical underpinning of free trade.

NEW TRADE THEORY

New trade theory has also suggested that the theory of comparative advantage is not as important as previously first thought. New trade theory states that the key thing in modern production is not comparative advantage but economies of scale. With industries operating on a global scale, increasing the size of any manufacturing process can lead to substantial savings through economies of scale, which reduce average costs. Therefore, the key thing is choosing to specialize in a particular industry and gaining as many economies of scale as possible. The initial comparative advantage may not be that important.

Another aspect of new trade theory is that the biggest gains to trade come from trading with near neighbours. This is due not just to lower transport costs, but also to shared cultural, social and economic values. For example, European clothes producers will have a good understanding of European fashion sentiments that might be hard to replicate for Asian producers. For low-cost budget clothes, the comparative advantage will continue to lie with manufacturers in Southeast Asia. But, for more fashionable items, it is not so much price that is important but the quality and ability to meet consumer preferences.

LIMITS TO COMPARATIVE ADVANTAGE

There are further limits to comparative advantage. Firstly, the theory assumes frictionless trade. In practice, there will be some barriers to trade. In recent years, firms have begun to re-evaluate where they produce. In 2021, this was in response to transport costs rising due to COVID-related supply chain issues. In 2022, it was in response to the Russian invasion of Ukraine. The year 2022 has seen a growth in reshoring as companies bring production back closer to domestic markets.

The principle of comparative advantage can also be influenced by tariff barriers and embargoes, which can result in retaliation and a fall in trade, leading to the loss of the potential gains of comparative advantage.

New trade theory

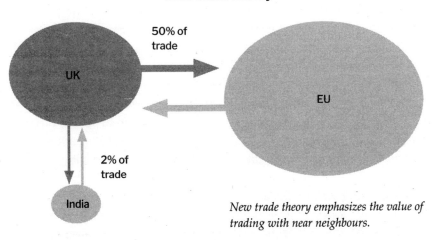

New trade theory emphasizes the value of trading with near neighbours.

33
Globalization

Globalization is the process of increased integration of the world economy.

Whereas in the past, national economies were largely self-reliant, globalization has led to increased trade and economic interdependence between countries all around the world. This process of globalization has also led to greater movement of labour and capital as people and businesses no longer feel constrained by national boundaries. Globalization has been part of social evolution for many centuries; it is not just a twentieth-century phenomenon. But the past 100 years have seen a turbocharging of globalization, with most industries becoming deeply integrated into the world economy. When people ask where a car was made, we can no longer pinpoint one country because its constituent parts will have come from several countries.

Globalization creates both threats and opportunities. The growth in trade has been a major factor in reducing poverty rates across the world – especially in Asia. In fact, the reduction in absolute poverty rates is one of the unheralded success stories of the past 50 years, and the process of globalization can take some credit for this. Yet, globalization is also feared for the threat that it has damaged local industry and jobs by outsourcing production across the globe. Globalization has also been linked to environmental problems such as the global demand for non-renewable resources and the pollution arising from increased output.

Container ships benefit from large economies of scale.

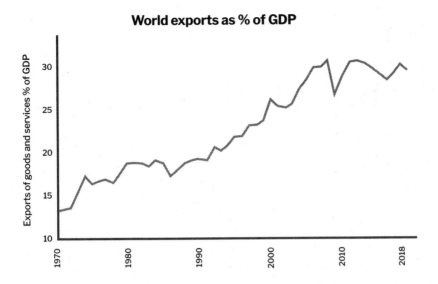

World exports as % of GDP

FORCES BEHIND GLOBALIZATION

Since World War II, there has largely been peace and prosperity within the major economies. This has encouraged firms to seek to expand markets overseas. Improved technology and transport links have made international trade more effective. Even something like the humble transport container was very influential in cutting costs of trade and making it much more economical. In fact, transporting goods and components has been so cheap that firms increasingly specialize production around the world. An Apple iPhone, for example, is made of several components, which are produced in factories across the globe. The GPS device may be made in Switzerland and the screen in China, while development takes place in the United States. In fact, the list of countries involved in the manufacture of the iPhone is quite long; it is truly a global product. Another factor behind globalization is the growth of trading blocks such as the European Union, NAFTA and AFTA (in Southeast Asia), which have increased regional integration.

PROBLEMS OF GLOBALIZATION

Globalization has generated many critics. Firstly, not everyone is happy with the spread of powerful multinational companies, claiming it has led to the demise of some local business who cannot compete, which in turn has led to a decline in cultural diversity. More problematic, the big shifts involved in globalization have put some industries out of business, leading to structural unemployment. For example, in the US

Impact of globalization

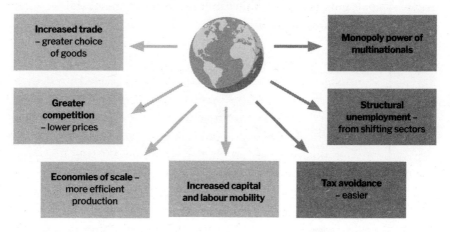

and Europe, globalization is blamed as the cause of unemployment in old manufacturing industries, and this hit unskilled, manual labour hard. In theory, this unemployment should be solved by new jobs created by globalization. But, in practice, it is difficult for those left behind by globalization to seamlessly transition to new areas of growth, and it is these structural problems which have created vocal critics.

It is often reported that multinationals bring investment and growth, but there are downsides: their influence and size means they can put pressure on governments to cut corporation tax rates or offer tax breaks. The past 50 years of globalization have seen a steady fall in global corporation tax rates and a growth in tax avoidance, with multinationals such as Amazon and Apple now adept at hiding profit and revenue in tax havens, meaning the average taxpayer is losing out from the benefits of globalization.

Another criticism of globalization is that it has accelerated many of the world's environmental problems. The growth of trade has led to ever-rising demand for natural commodities and their extraction has led to resource depletion and external impacts on the environment.

A final problem of globalization is that the greater movement of people and capital has led to unfortunate side effects. There has been increased demand for living in certain key cities, such as London and New York. The free movement of capital has caused property prices in these areas to increase substantially. This has caused inequality, with key workers struggling to buy or rent housing. Conversely, globalization can cause an outflow of skilled labour from low-income countries as they seek higher wages and more opportunities abroad. When the most skilled workers leave a developing economy, this can limit its entrepreneurial capacity and lead to lower opportunities for the poorer, developing economies.

IN DEFENCE OF GLOBALIZATION

Some economists argue that these criticisms are based on a mis-understanding. It is true that the world faces many environmental problems, but the solution is not to reverse the process of globalization but to ensure the right incentives and policies are in place to mitigate these problems. You could argue, in fact, that environmental issues highlight the need for a global response to these issues. It is no use trying to deal with global warming on a country-by-country basis; the issue requires global cooperation to reduce carbon emissions.

While the process of globalization has led to some temporary structural unemployment, this is not a new economic phenomenon and has been a feature of capitalist economies for many centuries. Trying to stop globalization wouldn't protect workers from all these changes in the economy. Instead we should put more focus on all the benefits of globalization, such as increased trade, lower prices and the economies of scale from increased global production. Also, it is a myth that global-ization does not help developing economies. While they may lose some skilled labour, this usually leads to an increase in remittances (money flows) back to family members. Globalization has been a key factor in lifting many out of poverty due to the gains possible from trade, capital inflows and the equalizing of living standards.

New York has become a major international city in the globalized world.

34

Tariffs and Free Trade

In previous centuries tariffs on imported goods were often a major source of government revenue.

In the early eighteenth century a surprising 95% of US federal revenue came from import duties. It was a convenient source of income for the government and taxing foreign producers was often politically easier than taxing domestic consumers and workers. However, high tariffs discourage trade and can leave the average person worse off. Economists tend to agree that free trade can lead to an increase in economic welfare, even if non-economists sometimes remain unconvinced.

The logic behind free trade is that reducing tariffs on imports means that consumers (and firms) will see a decrease in prices and an effective increase in disposable income. Because it is cheaper to buy imports,

Tariffs can reduce trade and lead to a loss of welfare for consumers.

A Samsung factory in 1985. South Korea used tariffs in the 20th century to protect its infant industries.

consumers will be able to spend more on other items. Therefore, although it may not be obvious, some domestic firms will see an increase in demand because consumers now have more purchasing power. The important thing about free trade is that the country will be better off from unilaterally reducing import tariffs – even where other countries don't also cut tariffs. However, usually when one country cuts import duties, other countries will agree to reciprocate and also reduce theirs. Therefore, exporting firms who have a comparative advantage will also see a growth in demand, creating new jobs. Free trade tends to cause a shift in production from inefficient industries to more efficient industries, but overall the economy should be better off.

It is true that some domestic industries may lose out. Firms that are internationally uncompetitive may require tariff protection to be able to stay in business. When tariffs are reduced, they cannot compete and go out of business. This is why there can be so much political pressure for governments to keep tariffs. However, while certain sectors may benefit from tariffs, the wider economy does not. Cutting tariffs can enable the growth of new industries which have a comparative advantage. Free trade has been an important factor in promoting economic growth around the world, especially in Southeast Asia.

However, while free trade can be shown to increase net economic welfare, it is not universally seen to be beneficial, and it is quite possible that some countries benefit from free trade more than others.

For example, at the present time, the comparative advantage of many developing economies may be situated in producing primary products – raw material extraction, food crops. Therefore, the logic of free trade is that developing countries should specialize in these basic industries. However, this could be damaging in the long term. These industries can be volatile (with fluctuations in price causing fluctuations in income) and they leave limited room for economic growth and increase in real wages. A rise in global incomes leads not to the purchase of more commodities like food, but rather to the purchase of higher-value-added goods, like electronics.

A developing economy may therefore feel that in the long term it would be desirable to diversify and develop a new industrial base, which gives scope for higher productivity and economic growth. However, without tariffs, these new industries would never be able to get established because it will always be cheaper to buy imports. Therefore, a temporary period of tariffs can enable these 'infant industries' to gain some experience and at least be able to sell to the domestic market. As they develop and gain economies of scale, the need for tariffs will reduce, and over time tariffs can be cut. Therefore, there is a strong case for developing economies to have the option of some limited tariffs. Advanced economies, including the UK, the US and South Korea, all had periods of tariff protection at some stage in their economic development. Insisting on free trade for everyone else has been likened to 'kicking away the ladder that you used to climb up'.

Another factor about tariffs is that we shouldn't discount the real hardship that can occur from removing them. If their removal causes an industry to close down, this will lead to structural unemployment and likely regional decline in the area where the industry was located. It may be true that overall the economy gains, but these gains are spread thinly across a large population, and the losses are felt much more keenly by a small section of the population. In certain circumstances, economists may be sympathetic to temporary tariffs to give an industry the chance to reinvent itself. But they will also be aware that once 'temporary' tariffs have been introduced, it can be very difficult to remove them.

Nevertheless, resorting to tariffs in difficult times usually exacerbates the situation. A good example is the introduction of tariffs during the Great Depression, which led to a further

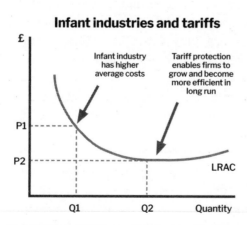

Developing economies may need protection before they can expand production.

shrinking of world trade. By 1930, many industries in the United States were seeing a collapse in demand due to bank failures and falling money supplies. Industry leaders and workers saw one potential solution in tariffs to stop cheap imports and increase the domestic market. US Congress responded by passing the Smoot–Hawley Tariff Act, which imposed very high tariffs on many imports. The problem is that this increased prices for consumers, who were already struggling to make ends meet. Faced with higher import prices, they cut back on other expenditures. Also, the lurch towards protectionism encouraged a wave of protectionism around the world as other countries tried to protect their own domestic industries. As a result, US exporting firms now found new barriers to trade and saw a slump in export demand. In trying to prop up some domestic industries, the Act ironically caused other export industries to fail. Most economists agree that protectionism exacerbated the length and depth of the Great Depression.

35
The Euro

The Euro is the official currency of 19 member states in the European Union. It is the world's largest single currency and includes a diverse range of countries who all share the same currency and monetary policy.

Introduced in 1999, the Euro was designed to reduce transaction costs, eliminate exchange rate uncertainty and encourage greater integration of the European economy. However, while the single currency has many benefits, it also created unexpected problems as divergent economies struggled to cope with the same exchange rate and monetary policy.

ADVANTAGES OF THE SINGLE CURRENCY

The main advantage of the Euro is that it avoids unnecessary transaction costs in exchanging currency. European economies are closely integrated with the free movement of labour and capital across national borders. The single currency makes this much easier and prevents the costs of currency conversion and loose change. For firms and business, another significant advantage is that it eliminates uncertainty over exchange rate fluctuations. For example, if a Belgian firm imported raw materials from Spain and exported to Germany, its business profits would be affected by swings in the exchange rate. However, using the Euro enables the firm to plan ahead, knowing that the exchange rate will not alter import costs or the price of exports. The combination of lower transaction costs and exchange rate certainty encourages firms to invest in the eurozone. For multinational firms,

The Euro: the world's largest single currency.

investing in the eurozone is also attractive precisely because it can benefit from direct access to a single market of 340 million citizens. Another potential advantage is that prices in Euros makes it easier for citizens to compare prices – and if companies overcharge in one country, it is relatively easy to buy from elsewhere in the eurozone.

DRAWBACKS OF THE SINGLE CURRENCY

Given all the benefits and undoubted convenience of the single currency, why are some countries reluctant to join? A single currency needs to have one central bank and a common monetary policy. There is only one interest rate for the whole eurozone area, which is set by the European Central Bank (ECB). If the economies are closely integrated and growing at a similar rate, this common monetary policy will not present any issues. However, in periods of divergence, it can become very problematic. In the boom years of 2000–07, the economies of Portugal, Greece and Spain became relatively uncompetitive. Productivity grew at a slower rate in southern than northern Europe, and as a consequence their exports became more expensive. The result was a relative fall in exports, a rise in demand for imports and a growing current account deficit.

Outside the Euro, a depreciation in the exchange rate would have enabled individual countries to restore competitiveness. But, in the Euro, this is not possible, so countries in southern Europe ended up with

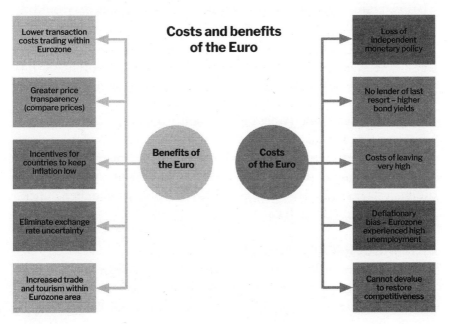

very large current account deficits. Further, uncompetitive economies made for lower economic growth and saw growing budget deficits. These countries had no central bank of their own to increase liquidity and buy bonds where necessary. So in addition to the current account deficit, Greece, Portugal and Spain saw rising bond yields, and the ECB was unwilling to help. These countries were forced to pursue austerity – cutting government spending to reduce budget deficits and prevent rising bond yields. Therefore, southern Europe faced two problems: an overvalued exchange rate causing lower exports and austerity causing lower economic growth. The result was that the countries went into a deep recession.

Usually when a country enters a recession with low inflation and an overvalued exchange rate, its central bank will pursue looser monetary policy – cutting interest rates and/or increasing the money supply. However, this doesn't happen in the eurozone, because the ECB can't set different monetary policies for different countries. This is the big disadvantage of the Euro: monetary policy may be unsuitable for countries which are growing at a different rate to the eurozone average.

LEARNING FROM ECB MISTAKES

In 2012, the ECB were faced with a real crisis – rising bond yields, recession and uncompetitive countries. The ECB president at the time, Mario Draghi, announced that within its mandate the bank would do 'whatever it takes' to restore stability. This announcement helped calm market nerves and bond yields started to fall. However, it does mean that the ECB, an unelected central bank, has significant influence over different economies depending on how much it is willing to intervene. Some economists argue that for the single currency to fully work, the EU should seek common rules on fiscal policy and common Euro bonds. However, for political reasons, this is difficult and past fiscal rules about limiting government borrowing have frequently been broken. The eurozone still faces the potential problem that when countries are at different stages in the economic cycle, there are only very limited policies to help deal with the imbalances.

OPTIMAL CURRENCY ZONE

A key question for the Euro is the extent to which the eurozone is an optimal currency zone. An optimal currency zone is one where the benefits of a single currency outweigh the costs. For example, the United States is an optimal currency zone for a single currency – the dollar is used across 50 different states. Suppose that California entered a recession and was uncompetitive, but the East Coast was booming. The Federal Reserve can't have a different monetary policy for California, but it is relatively easy for Californian workers to move to the East Coast where better jobs are available. Therefore, regional differences don't matter because of the flexibility of labour and capital in moving between areas with a common language and nationality. However, whether the eurozone is an optimal currency zone is a more difficult question. When the Greek economy was in major recession with unemployment of 20%, there were practical difficulties for Greeks to move to Germany to find employment in booming industries. These included language and cultural barriers and the difficulty in gaining accommodation. Therefore, although free movement is theoretically possible, in practice, pockets of high unemployment exist.

36

Foreign Aid

Given widespread global inequality, it has been hoped that foreign aid can help redress this global imbalance, reduce poverty, tackle humanitarian crises and provide the capital to enable real progress in economic development.

However, the merits of foreign aid have often been questioned, critics arguing that aid rarely targets the most worthwhile projects but is subject to political pressures and the need to benefit the donor country too. There is also a concern that aid can encourage dependency, and the argument is that promoting trade and internal growth of the developing economies is a better strategy.

BENEFITS OF AID

Firstly, when a developing economy is overwhelmed by a natural disaster or war, they lack the resources to cope with the humanitarian crisis. Aid can play a crucial role in helping developing economies get through a crisis and avoid the unnecessary loss of human life. In the longer term, developing economies can get stuck in a cycle of low capital investment leading to low economic growth, which means that the necessary investment is not forthcoming. Foreign aid can bypass this inability to finance and borrow for investment and provide capital infrastructure directly. Aid can also help a developing economy deal with market failure. For example, infrastructure and education are public goods that a free market will fail to provide. The problem is that many developing economies struggle to gain sufficient tax revenues to finance these public services.

For example, foreign aid which enables the building of roads, schools and hospitals can improve the infrastructure of an economy, not only providing an important public service but also enabling higher productivity and economic growth in the long term. In some models of economic growth (such as the Harrod–Domar growth model), the amount

Vietnam developed primarily through trade.

of capital investment is considered an important factor in determining long-run growth. Aid that leads to capital flows can improve the balance of payments, increase a nation's wealth and provide a kick-start to economic growth. Aid can also take the form of debt forgiveness, which can hold back developing economies because the spending on debt interest payments reduces the amount of government funds available for other more worthwhile projects.

TRADE, NOT AID

Critics argue that most aid takes the form of tied aid, where a donor gives aid in return for deals to purchase goods and services from the donor countries. One issue around foreign aid is that the biggest recipients of aid are not always the poorest countries, but middle-ranking economies who purchase considerable exports from the donor country. For example, in 2018, the UK gave £71m in aid to China despite China having an economy five times as large as the UK. Another problem for aid is the scope for corruption and syphoning off aid for non-humanitarian purposes. A study by the Elite Capture of Foreign Aid found one-sixth of foreign aid to 22 countries ended up in tax havens like Switzerland.

Another concern about foreign aid is that aid in the form of healthcare spending, say, creates a temptation for the developing economy's government to cut back its own spending on healthcare and spend more on their military instead. Therefore, the flow of aid creates its own need to continue the funding, because the basic healthcare services set up will not be able to meet minimum service standards without the flow of foreign aid. If healthcare is provided directly by the developing economy, it becomes more durable because it is not reliant on receiving foreign aid. Given the potential problems of reliance, some economists

Trade vs aid

Trade	Aid
Free trade – powerful force to increase economic welfare and living standards.	Infant industry argument – free trade can be unfair. Tariffs can help economies diversify.
Problems of aid – given for the wrong reasons can distort democracy.	Increase capital – aid can fill in capital shortages and break the cycle of low growth/low savings.
Displacement effects – foreign aid can displace local incentives to develop comprehensive public services, e.g. healthcare.	Market failure – aid can help deal with market failure – e.g. in transport and education. Aid can complement free markets.
Poverty reduction in Southeast Asia – the decline in absolute poverty levels in China and Asia came from trade, not aid.	Crisis relief – aid is necessary for overcoming crises, such as war, famine and natural disaster.

argue that the best policy is to encourage trade and self-sufficiency among developing economies. Proponents of free trade argue that the reduction in poverty comes from economic growth and the development of more efficient export industries. For example, in China and Southeast Asia, the past few decades have seen a remarkable decline in poverty, not through foreign aid, but through trade and economic growth. The advantage is that the government of the developing economy can then choose how to use the proceeds of economic growth, and is not tied to the wishes of the donor countries.

NEED FOR AID

However, these criticisms of aid may be exaggerated. Not all countries have benefitted from trade and globalization like China and Vietnam. In particular, sub-Saharan Africa does not have the same infrastructure which has enabled the growth of manufacturing export industries. While Southeast Asia has posted record growth rates, sub-Saharan Africa has fallen behind. With poor rates of economic growth, foreign aid can help tackle some of the shortfalls in development. Corruption is a problem for many developing economies, but there is no evidence that aid is always wasted. Given in the right way, aid can be seen to provide public infrastructure which does give long-term benefits. Also, another problem with relying on free trade is that the benefits of free trade do not always flow to the poorest economies. The logic of free trade may mean that a developing economy gets stuck producing raw commodities because that is where their comparative advantage lies. But if a developing economy produces only raw commodities and fossil fuels, there is very limited scope for economic growth and development into higher-value-added industries. To compensate for the inequality of free trade agreements, foreign aid can provide capital to help diversify the economy and make it less reliant on volatile raw commodities.

A big issue for foreign aid is how it is given and what form it takes. The best form of aid empowers local communities to make their own decisions and investments. For example, microfinancing is a form of aid which gives interest-free loans to the poorest (often women) in society. These loans are very small scale and have to be paid back, but this makes sure that people take out the loans only if they feel they can make them work. In a way the aid is solving the problem of market failure where banks fail to lend to the poorest. The advantage of these schemes is that they unlock the productive capacity of the local population and rely on local knowledge, rather than top-down spending from wealthy economies. This form of aid is more sustainable because it rewards local enterprise.

Microfinance lends money to individuals which they would not be able to obtain otherwise.

37

Inequality

There are many different types of inequality – income inequality, wealth inequality and inequality between nations.

A key question is to what extent inequality is a necessary and even desirable ingredient of capitalism. There is no easy answer, but the rise in inequality of the past few decades does raise difficult questions.

ROLE OF INEQUALITY

Firstly, some communist economies did seek to impose equality of outcome on society, but this came at a high cost. Firstly, it reduced incentives for workers and businesses to take risks, innovate and work hard. Also, the mechanism of ensuring equality required significant state intervention, which became ripe for corruption and so created a different kind of inequality. In a market economy, the prospect of profit and higher earnings is a key motivating factor for entrepreneurs to set

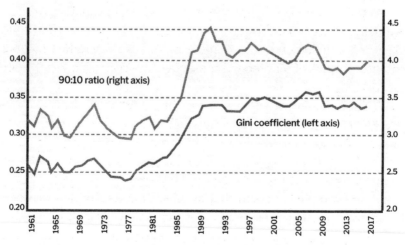

Inequality in the UK – the Gini coefficient and the 90:10 ratio

Inequality rose in the UK in the 1980s.

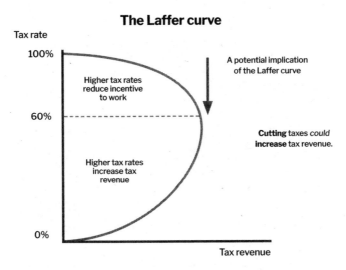

The Laffer curve

Tax rate

100%

Higher tax rates reduce incentive to work

60%

Higher tax rates increase tax revenue

0%

A potential implication of the Laffer curve

Cutting taxes *could* **increase** tax revenue.

Tax revenue

up a business, and potentially create jobs and income that will ultimately benefit the whole society. Without this incentive, economies tend to stagnate with little innovation and little risk-taking.

In countries with very high marginal rates of taxation, there is a risk that workers will cut back on overtime, find ways to avoid tax and even move to another country. For example, in 2012 the French government announced a top rate marginal income tax of 75% on incomes over €1 million. The aim was to reduce inequality, but the high tax rate generated a disappointing amount of tax revenue because many high-profile workers and business sought to register in low tax rate economies such as Belgium. In a globalized world, it is easy to avoid high tax rates.

At the other end of the spectrum, a concern of free market economists is that generous benefits may discourage the unemployed from taking a job or working longer hours. Benefits to the poor can reduce inequality, but there is a risk of unintended consequences – namely, lower incentives to work.

A controversial idea behind inequality is known as the trickle-down effect – the argument that when the wealthy become wealthier, everyone in society benefits because the increased wealth and high incomes also gives benefits to other people. As long as everyone is better off, it shouldn't matter if the relative gap between rich and poor increases. Take, for example, a tax cut that increases the wealth of a rich person by $1 million. They are now in a position to consume more goods and employ more servants, which will lead to higher wages in the economy, so benefitting others.

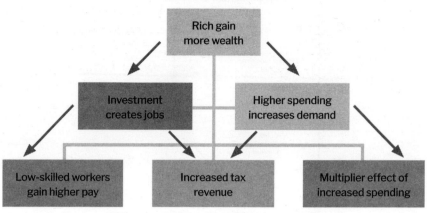

The trickle-down effect

However, the trickle-down effect is disputed. Firstly, if the rich gained an extra $1 million, very little may trickle down to other workers. The rich have a high marginal propensity to save, and may put all the $1 million in a bank account or buy property. Far from increasing average wages, this just inflates the price of assets such as houses, making it more difficult for those on low incomes to afford housing. Also, it is sometimes assumed that extremes of wealth are caused because entrepreneurs work hard or have great skill to set up a business. But inequality of wealth often occurs through inheritance or the use of monopoly power. In this case, inequality is rewarding not hard work but rather a lucky position in society. For example, a firm with significant monopoly power can raise prices for consumers and also pay low wages, enabling the firm to make more profit. In theory, higher profit could bring the benefit of higher taxes paid. But, this profit may be hidden from the government by paying higher salaries or bonuses or depositing it in overseas bank accounts that don't attract corporation tax.

There are other drawbacks of inequality. Firstly, there is the diminishing marginal utility of wealth. If a millionaire gains more income, the increase in his satisfaction/happiness is very limited. If a person on the breadline gains more income, this makes a significant difference to their standard of living. When comparing GDP per capita between countries, it is important to take into account the distribution of income. For example, the GDP per capita of the Middle Eastern countries Qatar and Saudi Arabia is very high, suggesting they are the wealthiest countries in the world. But this average GDP per capita masks very large levels of inequality. With the majority of GDP owned by a small share of the population, a more

High GDP per capita may mask high levels of inequality within society.

useful measure is something like median incomes. This takes the income of the population in the middle of the income distribution spectrum and is not skewed by the very high levels of the richest 1%.

Another point to remember about inequality is that people who gain some increase in income will not necessarily be happy to become relatively poorer. Behavioural economics tells us that relative worth is very important (see pages 170–3). If we see the rest of society becoming much richer and feel that we are missing out, this causes a sense of ill will. Therefore, widespread inequality can be a source of social unrest.

It is also important to consider the type of inequality. Wealth inequality has increased in recent decades because there is a strong degree of wealth being passed on to future generations. Tax on wealth is very low compared to income, partly because it is harder to tax wealth without avoidance schemes. But wealth itself can easily beget more wealth. For example, purchasing assets like housing, shares and bonds, gives the owner a steady income stream that can be reinvested in buying more. Those on low incomes rarely have the luxury of being able to invest in order to increase their wealth. Also, the wealthy can benefit from rising property prices. Thomas Piketty argues that wealth grows faster than economic growth, using the expression $r > g$ where r is the rate of return to wealth and g, economic growth. This is because the wealthy can reinvest dividends and rental incomes to accumulate even more wealth.

Thomas Piketty.

38
Minimum Wages

A minimum wage is a legal wage floor within an economy. Most major economies have some form of minimum wage.

In the United States, the Federal minimum wage is $7.25 an hour, though some states pay up to $15. In Europe, the minimum wage can vary from €36 per month in Bulgaria to €2,313 a month in Luxembourg. The minimum wage is designed to increase incomes of the low paid, reduce poverty and encourage firms to increase labour productivity. Critics of a minimum wage argue it raises business costs, reduces employment and can make some industries uncompetitive.

ARGUMENTS FOR MINIMUM WAGES

The main argument for a minimum wage is that it raises the income of the lowest-paid workers and helps to reduce in-work poverty. In the absence of minimum wages, firms with monopsony power (the ability to set wages through their domination of the market) are able to pay

Annual minimum wages in major industrial economies

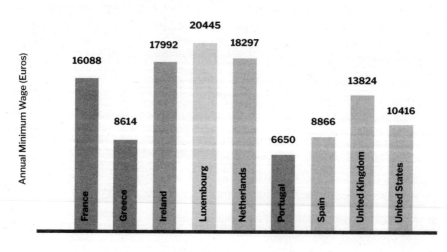

wages below the equilibrium and make excess profit at the expense of workers' incomes. Many workers have limited bargaining power and, if offered a low-paid job, will find it difficult to simply move to a higher-paid, more competitive job, so minimum wages can help to increase fairness within an economy. The role of the minimum wage has become more important with the relative decline in the power of trade unions, leaving workers with little ability to bargain for higher wages.

Another important argument for a minimum wage is that by seeking to promote a higher wage economy, it encourages firms to invest in new technology and working practices that can increase labour productivity. If the cost of labour rises, firms will wish to get more output from each worker and so invest in the technology that raises output per worker. In the long term, this can benefit the economy because it leads to a higher value added per worker and not just a competition for the lowest wages.

Another possible benefit of the minimum wage is that increasing the incomes of the lowest paid will raise demand in the economy because workers are likely to spend any of the increase in their wages on rent and goods and services.

Another feature of the minimum wage is that it will push up all wages in an industry, making it easier for firms to absorb the wage increases by increasing prices. For example, an increase in the minimum wage is likely to have a big impact on fast food restaurants. But, since all the big firms are equally affected, it is likely price rises will be sufficient for firms to pay the higher costs.

A final benefit of minimum wages is that it can reduce the cost of in-work benefit. For example, in the United Kingdom, those on low wages are eligible for Universal Credit to help households meet basic living costs. A higher minimum wage would reduce the need for government benefits.

PROBLEMS OF MINIMUM WAGES

The main problem of a minimum wage is that it may discourage firms from hiring workers, especially vulnerable workers in the lowest-paid industries. It is argued that rapid increases in the

Milton Friedman.

minimum wage will cause unemployment to rise as firms get rid of workers rather than pay the higher wages. This was the belief of Milton Friedman, who argued in 1966: 'Many well-meaning people favor legal minimum-wage rates in the mistaken belief that they help the poor. These people confuse wage rates with wage income.' It was Friedman's contention that the minimum wage would hurt the unskilled in particular by taking away their chance to have on-the-job training through employment. Another danger of a minimum wage is that it could encourage firms to take on workers in the grey economy and to find ways to avoid paying them the legal minimum.

LABOUR AS A COMMODITY

One thing about the debate on minimum wages is that critics of a minimum wage can apply a simple supply and demand diagram – what you might call Economics 101. A higher price of cars causes a fall in demand, so by extension a higher price for labour will also cause a fall in demand. However, labour markets are often more complex than goods markets. One observation of a minimum wage is that when wage rates go up, workers can become more motivated and increase their productivity. A higher-paid job is more desirable, so the worker is keener to keep the job. With higher wages, we get lower labour turnover, and this helps to reduce costs for business. Higher wages can also motivate people to enter the labour force and increase the gap between benefits and wages.

Minimum wages

Wages

Supply of labour

Minimum wage

Equilibrium

Demand for labour

Unemployment   Employment

A minimum wage could, in theory, cause unemployment.

Advanced economies such as the United Kingdom and United States often have shortage of labour in 'unpopular' jobs, such as fruit pickers and cleaners. Raising wages can motivate people to enter the labour force and take a job that they otherwise would have refused.

The effect of minimum wages on employment is an issue that often divides economists. Empirical studies show both that it can cause unemployment and that the effect on employment is statistically insignificant. Yet, in the UK, there has been a significant increase in the minimum wage since 1997 (above inflationary growth) – and unemployment at the end of 2022 is close to full employment (3.8%). This shows that over time minimum wage increases can be absorbed by the economy without a major adverse impact on either employment or unemployment.

39
Behavioural Economics

The traditional model of economics assumed that the average individual was rational and sought to maximize their economic welfare.

Firms sought to maximize profits, while consumers sought to maximize their income and purchase the optimal combination of goods and services. This is a model of utility theory, and utilitarian philosophers like J.S. Mill and Jeremy Bentham were also interested in economics, so it is no surprise that the model found its way into economics. Further, there is some logic to the assumption – in a very broad sense, we do consume in accordance with utility – and it definitely makes the development of economic models and theories easier. However, after 150+ years of economic thought came the realization that individuals are not always rational but subject to a large array of human biases, prejudices and irrational thinking, leading to unexpected behaviour. Initially, a lot of these new insights came not from economists but from psychologists who used their knowledge in an economic setting. But this new branch of economics is now widely accepted and is a significant development in the subject.

RATIONAL PRICING

There is a theory of markets known as rational pricing. The argument is that a market price of a stock or commodity should reflect its true value because otherwise there is a profit incentive to take advantage of the difference between its true value and real value. In this theory, prices should not be subject to irrational over- or undervaluation because this would enable an investor to

Jeremy Bentham.

In the Netherlands in the 17th century, tulip bulb prices reached extraordinary highs. The phenomenon, known as 'Tulip Mania', was satirized by Jan Brueghel the Younger in this 1640 painting.

make profit. However, in the real world, we do see irrational behaviour and booms and bust in asset prices. For example, in the early 2000s, US house prices rose above their long-term value. They rose not only faster than inflation and economic growth, but faster than average earnings. By historical standards they were overvalued on every measure. However, at the time, many analysts were confident that this time things were different, and gave reasons to explain the historical anomalies.

However, between 2006 and 2009 prices crashed, showing that it had been a housing bubble all along. A large majority of individuals can indeed be irrational for a long time. Firstly, we can be subject to optimism bias. When prices are rising, homeowners, estate agents and bankers are all happy to believe prices will keep rising. To warn prices are overvalued could make an advisor unpopular and lose them business. As the saying goes: 'I'd rather be wrong with the majority than right with the minority.' This optimism bias, or irrational exuberance, is related to the concept of herd mentality. If the majority of people are saying tech stocks will keep rising or that tulip bulbs are a great investment, we tend to go along with the majority – thinking they must know something we don't.

Behavioural economics can have important insights in many fields. For example, it was once assumed that the best way to motivate people was money – pay bonuses to workers, pay for good behaviour. However, some studies have found that paying workers a bonus for doing extra can soon become counterproductive. What workers really value is not a financial bonus but being appreciated or having a sense of responsibility at work.

Another interesting example comes from Israel, where a new rule was introduced to fine parents who collected their children late from school. The expectation was that a financial penalty would create an incentive to pick up on time. But actually the opposite happened. After paying a small fine, parents felt less guilty about being late. In other words, the penalty or tax can change our behaviour in unexpected ways.

NUDGE THEORY

Governments are increasingly using behavioural economics to change our behaviour in subtle ways. We may or may not be aware of this. Nudge theory suggests we can easily be encouraged to make certain decisions through small changes to the presentation of choices. For example, if you have to opt in to a pension scheme, the take-up rate is quite low. If you have to opt out, and opting out requires filling in many forms and takes time, the take-up rate increases dramatically. Note that the outcome of these contrasting behaviours is the same. A rational person should, in theory, behave the same way in either circumstance. But a key factor in behaviour is something called default choices. We often take the path of least resistance; we don't have the time to weigh up every decision like the rational individual of an economics textbook. Similarly, to be an organ donor you may need to carry a card. But an alternative approach is to require a card specifying that you refuse to be an organ donor. In other words, you specifically have to opt out. This definitely increases the number of people 'choosing' to be a donor.

In its workplace, Google used to place M&Ms in open baskets. But then they tried putting them in bowls with lids. This small change reduced the number of M&Ms consumed by 3 million a month. This probably comes as no surprise – when it's easy to snack, the human brain tends to choose the immediate reward, but make

Simply adding a lid to bowls of M&Ms led to significantly reduced consumption.

Social media companies may 'nudge' us through notifications and clickbait content in a less positive approach.

it a little more difficult and our choices are very different. This kind of impulsive behaviour was never captured by standard economic theory.

THE CONTROVERSY OF NUDGE THEORY

While these examples may appear benign, it is easy for this nudge theory to become less palatable. For example, social media companies know there are certain secrets of human psychology which can trap consumers in behaviours that reduce their quality of life. Facebook and others have been very successful in creating apps that users constantly feel a need to check. Red notification buttons grab our attention, pushing 'clickbait' content that is hard to dismiss and which keeps us scrolling. Many people admit to using social media more than they would like. It doesn't make them genuinely happy, but the companies' business model is based on keeping us on the site for as long as possible.

This is not to say individuals are completely irrational. In fact, sometimes it is rational to cut corners, not to evaluate every decision but to keep life simple. However, when formulating economic models and predicting behaviour, it is important to bear in mind that most people may behave irrationally for quite a long time. From Tulip mania in the seventeenth century to the craze for tech stocks in the 1990s, there have been many booms and busts in asset prices, and there will probably be many more – just be careful of following the herd!

40
Moral Hazard

Moral hazard is a situation where an individual has an incentive to take a risky action because the cost is borne by other people.

For example, if your property is fully insured, you will feel less necessity of making sure it doesn't get damaged. If your phone is fully insured, you may be willing to take it on a roller coaster to get an action shot. If you drop the phone, the insurance company pays. But, if it wasn't insured, you wouldn't take the risk.

This is a problem for insurance companies because if they offer full insurance, consumer behaviour is likely to change, and it makes insurance much more expensive than it should be with normal risk-averse behaviour. In the worst case, firms may not be willing to provide insurance at all. This is the reason insurance companies will avoid giving 100% insurance but instead require people to pay a compulsory excess

Moral hazard

Excess risk-taking leads to bank losses

Risk-taking by banks

Government bailouts encourage risk-taking

Government bailout Government 'can't allow' banks to go bust

Moral hazard is when people are encouraged to take risks.

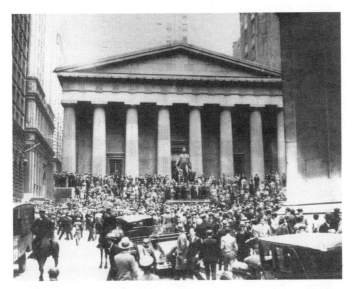

The Wall Street Crash, 24 October 1929.

fee of say £50 per each insurance claim. This compulsory excess (plus all the bureaucracy of making a claim) is enough to make sure consumers take sufficient care when using their insured products.

MORAL HAZARD IN BANKING

Perhaps the most dangerous example of moral hazard occurs in the banking sector. For various reasons governments have stated that they will protect the deposits of consumers in banks. There is a good logic for this. If consumers know their bank deposits are safe, no matter what, then we will all have confidence in the banking system, which will prevent a 'run on the bank' where people try to withdraw all their cash before the bank goes bankrupt. This 'run on the bank' happened in the United States in the 1930s during the Great Depression. Stock market falls caused people to withdraw money from the bank, but banks didn't have enough cash to meet the demand. This led to a loss of confidence and long queues as people sought to withdraw their money. Over 500 banks went bankrupt, causing people to lose their savings. After that experience, the US government has always promised to protect savings, with the Federal Reserve acting as 'lender of last resort'. However, if banks know they will be bailed out by the government, there is an incentive to take risky financial decisions. For an individual banker, if they take a risk and it works out, they may get a large bonus. However, if it fails, then it is someone else's problem. The bank may go bankrupt, requiring a bailout.

These perverse incentives were an important factor behind the Global Financial Crisis, which began with the credit crunch of 2008. In the early 2000s, many bankers and mortgage salesmen had personal incentives to take great risks, and for a few years they benefited from big bonuses as house prices rose and the number of new mortgages soared. However, this 'easy money' caused banks to take too many risks and eventually the bubble burst and the extent of bad loans in the system became known. Banks started to face a liquidity shock. To secure the financial systems, governments around the world had to bail out banks. Therefore, it was the ordinary taxpayer who paid the cost of the risks taken by private bankers.

MORAL HAZARD IN HEALTHCARE

Another example of moral hazard is in healthcare. In the UK, doctors in the NHS are aware of their budget. They know they have a limited budget and therefore need to ration healthcare. Therefore, they will not choose very expensive treatments that have only a very minimal chance of working or which offer only a minimal improvement in life quality. However, in the US system based on private insurance, doctors don't have any budget; the cost of treatment is paid for by outside insurance companies. Therefore, if a doctor feels a $1 million treatment may have only a 0.5% chance of working, he may still agree to the decision because he bears no direct cost. It is the insurance companies who will pay (and they probably will not know the poor chance of success). At first glance, we might think the US system is better because we would all like to try treatments even if they are expensive and unlikely to work. But, everything has an opportunity cost. Paying billions for unnecessary healthcare increases health premiums for everyone. The higher cost may mean some people are uninsured and don't get any treatment at all. This is why private health insurance companies may try to get more information about the benefit of treatment before agreeing to pay for it.

MORAL HAZARD IN GOVERNMENT

Another example of moral hazard could be in a government. A government official may take the decision to embark on a very expensive project, such as a high-speed train line, which is politically popular at the present time. However, if the project turns out in ten years' time to be a white elephant and a waste of money, the politician will not bear the cost. They are unlikely to be in power and it will be future taxpayers who have to pay.

A high-speed train line may be an example of moral hazard in government.

MORAL HAZARD IN THE ENVIRONMENT

Equally, as a society we may decide to ignore issues like global warming because we don't want to pay higher prices for gas and electricity. However, if our inaction causes global warming to accelerate, large parts of the world may be uninhabitable in the future. The problem is that our current decisions will be borne by future generations. We underplay future consequences because we do not directly face them. Moral hazard is a major problem when encouraging people to change their behaviour.

OVERCOMING MORAL HAZARD

To overcome moral hazard in banking, governments can make banks split up their operations so risky investment decisions are not tied to ordinary bank deposits. Therefore, a government doesn't guarantee everything a bank does – only consumer deposits. Also, if governments do have to bail out banks, there should be consequences for the bank directors who took bad decisions. If they have to pay financial penalties for losing money, they will be more careful about taking risks. The problem comes when they get bonuses for risks which pay off, but no cost for the risks which don't work out.

41
Modern Monetary Theory

MMT is an alternative macro-economic theory that states governments with control over currency should not be constrained by limits on government borrowing but create money to finance higher government spending.

The only constraint on increasing the money supply to finance spending is when the economy reaches full capacity and there are no spare resources.

MMT can work only in countries that issue their own currency and primarily borrow in their domestic currency. Examples include the United States, Japan, United Kingdom and Canada. Emerging economies like Argentina and Mexico, which borrow in foreign currency (dollars), cannot easily print money to finance the deficit, and this is why emerging economies often suffer debt crises. Creating money causes inflation and a devaluation in the currency, and the country then struggles to repay debt denominated in dollars. MMT also only works for a fiat currency – a currency not backed by assets like gold, meaning that a fixed amount of currency is in existence correlating to gold reserves. So MMT would not be possible under the Gold Standard (abandoned in the 1930s) or the

Modern Monetary Theory would not be possible under the Gold Standard.

Modern monetary theory has gained significant interest since the Financial Crisis of 2008 but still has many critics.

Bretton Woods system (developed after World War II and abandoned in 1971).

The radical nature of MMT is that governments shouldn't worry about deficits, and large government debt isn't a warning of collapse as some fiscal conservatives believe. Importantly, the government's budget should not be viewed like a household budget which has to balance at the end of the month because, unlike a household, the government can create money. MMT's adherents point to a country like Japan which has public sector debt over 200% of GDP, a situation that has been quite sustainable over recent decades with little inflation.

The logic behind MMT is that if there are spare resources in an economy, such as some unemployment, the government should print money and create employment – to build infrastructure, say. One practical use of MMT would be a government job guarantee. Unemployed workers actively seeking work, but unable to find a job, could be given a government-backed job, financed by money creation. By printing money, the government can finance the use of resources that would otherwise have been redundant. The only limit on money creation would be if there were no unemployed resources. In that situation, printing money would not lead to any notable increase in real output, but would cause inflation. The value of MMT theory is much more limited in times of inflation, because then printing money devalues the currency and limits any increase in real output.

In MMT, borrowing itself could become redundant. Rather than selling bonds to the private sector, the government could just create money and finance spending directly. Another aspect of MMT is that it prefers the interest rate set by the central bank to be 0% because issuing bonds that bear interest is unnecessary. This would be quite radical because zero interest rates would significantly redistribute income and wealth from savers to borrowers.

If interest rates are kept at zero, inflation can by fought by a combination of taxes and/or the regulation of excess monopoly power. For example, if inflation is increasing, governments should avoid using monetary policy, and instead raise taxes to withdraw excess demand. In the MMT model monetary policy is swapped for fiscal policy. Some MMTs also argue that inflation is not just due to excess demand but can also be the result of monopolies increasing profit margins, or booms in asset prices, which might require government regulation to prevent price gouging.

MMT was a relatively obscure economic model until the Great Financial Crisis of 2008. Then global economies went into recession and interest rates were cut to close to zero. In this climate, central banks in the UK and US were able to create money through quantitative easing (see pages 133–4) to finance part of government borrowing, and inflation remained very low. This experience suggests that in the right climate, the theory is correct: increasing the money supply to finance deficits is fine. However, this period of zero interest rates was a historical anomaly that has no real precedent in the twentieth century. In 2021–22, inflation rose to above 10% in many Western economies, due to excess demand in the United States and cost-push factors, such as rising oil prices. In this climate, the contention that governments don't have to worry about deficits is different. Printing money would exacerbate inflationary pressures and could easily cause an acceleration of inflationary pressure.

To some extent, much of MMT theory has similarities with Keynesian economics – the idea that in a recession, governments should seek to put unemployed resources into use. Keynesians tend to suggest higher borrowing (though they can be open to money creation too). The main difference is that MMT emphasizes the creation of money rather than borrowing as a general policy. Some theorists believe that money creation could finance a really ambitious spending scheme such as $32 trillion for a single-payer, universal healthcare system.

However, many economists still criticize the fundamental logic of MMT, arguing that it is a mistake to argue that government spending

Can printing money be used to finance government spending or will it simply lead to inflation?

can be financed by money creation because it is too easy for this to lead to inflation. There are many examples in history of governments whose creation of money has led to rampant inflation, from Weimar Germany to Zimbabwe. It is true that a government like the United Kingdom can never technically default on its debt because it can print money to meet borrowing requirements. However, this can cause an inflationary default. Printing money devalues the present value of bonds and savings, reducing the value of savings for many in the economy. Although technically this avoids deflation, the effect is at least a partial default.

Also, the idea of relying on tax rises to reduce inflation is politically naïve: during periods of high inflation, governments may be ideologically opposed to tax rises and they may be reluctant to increase taxes sufficiently. Also, an interest rate of 0% will inflate asset prices and increase the value of assets for the wealthy. Finally, there are other concerns that increasing the money supply to finance government spending will crowd out the (potentially more efficient) private sector.

42
Happiness and Economics

Traditional economists usually make the assumption that higher incomes are correlated to greater happiness.

They actually prefer the term higher utility (from the philosophers of utilitarianism like Bentham and Mill). The logic is understandable: given a choice between low income and high income, the vast majority would choose to have more money because it enables us to purchase more goods and services, and in the short term at least we associate this with more happiness. In terms of national policy, this link between wealth and happiness has led to maximizing GDP as one of the priorities of economic policy. Again, it is understandable that countries with higher GDP tend to be more desirable places to live than countries with low GDP. However, in recent decades, economists have become increasingly aware that traditional measures of economic performance have ignored a much more fundamental question: are they increasing human happiness and human welfare?

In 1950, US real GDP was $2.186 trillion. In 2022, it was $19.727 trillion. Average incomes in the United States are nine times higher in 2022. The big question is: are people happier due to this increase in real GDP? It is when we ask this kind of question that we start to immediately see the limitations of GDP as a guide to living standards and well-being.

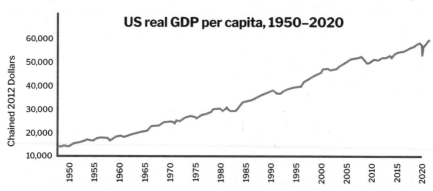

US real GDP per capita, 1950–2020

Firstly, it is quite difficult to quantify happiness. We can use surveys and ask people, but that makes for a very normative judgement. Another option is to look at indices which might increase happiness, including unemployment levels, the quality of housing, the amount of leisure time, the quality of the environment, life expectancy and education levels. When we start to direct economic policy towards happiness, it becomes much more complex and challenging than a one-dimensional goal of maximizing GDP and increasing our income.

DOES GDP INCREASE HAPPINESS?

Higher GDP does offer certain benefits for increasing happiness. For developing economies an increase in GDP has a strong correlation for reducing levels of absolute poverty. One hundred and fifty years ago, the wages of the poorest paid in both the United States and United Kingdom were barely sufficient to meet the minimum level of living. Economic growth has changed this for the better. In 1981, 40% of the world's population lived on less than $2.15 a day. By 2018, that had fallen to 8.7%. This is a real benefit of economic growth, which enables a reduction in the misery of absolute poverty. Higher GDP also enables economies to collect more tax and spend more on public services such as healthcare, education and potentially looking after the environment. These public services can improve life chances, education and happiness.

However, higher GDP is not guaranteed to increase happiness. With higher GDP, countries tend to experience higher levels of pollution and the whole world is grappling with the costs of global warming. Also, economic growth may create new problems, such as higher crime rates (more growth means that there are more goods to steal). A significant problem with recent growth is the increased congestion and pressure on land, which has been pushing up rental prices, especially in major cities. More wealth has been created, but its concentration in the hands of a small section of the population means that many households miss out on the benefits.

EASTERLIN PARADOX

According to research by Richard Easterlin, happiness usually increases as a poor country becomes richer. However, after a certain point of income, happiness fails to increase. In other words, we reach our sweet spot of happiness at a middle income – but after that, further increases do nothing to improve happiness. A lot of Easterlin's research was based on

Richard Easterlin.

The Easterlin paradox

Happiness

GDP

Higher GDP increases happiness up to a point.

the United States, where rising GDP has not led to higher reported levels of happiness. Why might happiness plateau with rising GDP?

Firstly, there is something known as the diminishing marginal utility of income. When you don't have enough money to buy food, extra income makes a huge improvement to your happiness. If you have $1 million a year, you are able to buy most things you could ever need. So it's unlikely that even a 20% raise would increase your happiness by enabling you to purchase more goods. If you bought yet another car, the increase in happiness is very limited.

PROBLEMS OF WEALTH

Another issue of wealth is that it brings its own problems. Higher living standards in the West have led to various problems of affluence – a rich, high-calorie diet and sedentary lifestyles have led to various health problems, such as obesity, diabetes and heart disease. Having more income is good, but if we are nudged into buying unhealthy foods, we suffer in the long run. Also, some countries have increased GDP through very long working weeks and a stressful working situation. We have more money, but not the time to enjoy it. At the other extreme, if you are super-rich and inherit money, you might not need to work and would have a lot of leisure time. But without any focus to life, you might squander the leisure time and end up consuming demerit goods (alcohol, drugs) which diminish your real satisfaction.

Back in 1930, the economist John Maynard Keynes forecast that technological progress would enable his grandchildren to work a 15-hour week and devote the remainder of their time to useful leisure pursuits. It was a utopian ideal based on the observation of technological progress. We have had the technological progress and productivity that could have enabled it, but unfortunately, such a utopian ideal still seems quite a long way off.

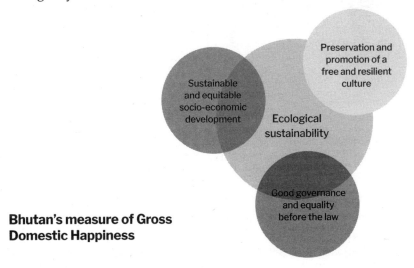

Bhutan's measure of Gross Domestic Happiness

RELATIVITY

Another issue with higher GDP is that a lot of people measure their success in relative terms. Am I better off than my neighbours? Rising GDP does nothing to change relative positions in society. It may even exacerbate inequality in society and make people feel they are missing out.

GROSS DOMESTIC HAPPINESS

An alternative measure of economic welfare is Gross Domestic Happiness (GDH). This involves a range of targets that influence a society's happiness. One of the nine is living standards (income), but others include cultural diversity, ecological diversity, environmental culture, good use of time, good governance and sustainable development. GDH was famously adopted by Bhutan in 2008 and is influenced by Buddhist concepts. In 2019 New Zealand ditched GDP for happiness and well-being. The new budget was based on improving mental health, reducing child poverty and transitioning to a low-emission, sustainable economy. Whatever the difficulties of incorporating happiness measures into economics, it is likely to grow in the future, as economics branches out away from traditional goals of income and profit maximization.

43
Externalities

An externality occurs when consuming or producing a product has an impact on a third party.

If we grow organic vegetables in our back garden, the costs and benefits will accrue almost entirely to ourselves; there is almost no effect on your neighbour. However, if a farmer grows vegetables through the use of pesticides and fertilizers, this production method could have costs to the rest of society. The pesticides designed to kill insects could, in the long term, damage Earth's ecosystem. Therefore, in the long term, there could be significant external costs from producing food with conventional farming. In a free market, these external costs are not included in the price, and therefore we can easily overproduce products which have these external costs. With externalities an important concept is that of social costs and social benefits. Social cost is private cost + external cost. For example, in the case of producing food, the private cost to a farmer of producing food is the raw materials and labour costs. But the social cost will include both these private costs plus the environmental external costs.

Pesticides can increase output, but cause pollution.

POSITIVE EXTERNALITIES

Externalities can also be positive. For example, if you decide to invest in learning a new skill at an evening class, you will get a benefit of improved qualifications and potentially a higher wage. However, improved training is not just a personal benefit; business and the wider economy will also benefit from a more educated workforce. Your decision to improve your workplace skills will help increase labour productivity and long-term economic growth. Therefore, we can say the social benefit of better education is greater than the private benefit. We can also see positive externalities in producing goods.

For example, if a major energy producer invested in renewable energies such as wind and solar, this would create positive externalities to society because providing renewable sources of energy will reduce carbon emissions from burning fossil fuels and reduce a country's dependence on the import of foreign energy.

An adult education class provides positive externalities.

WHY EXTERNALITIES MATTER

The problem is that when deciding what to produce and consume, individuals rarely take into account all externalities. For example, if you are deciding how to travel into a city centre, you weigh up the costs and benefits of how to travel and may decide to drive. However, if most people choose this decision, we end up with heavy traffic congestion, which imposes costs on everyone and leads to an inefficient outcome – we waste time, sitting in traffic jams. If we took into account externalities, a more socially efficient outcome would be to encourage other forms of transport – cycling, walking, public transport. To attain this more socially efficient outcome, it is necessary for a government to alter the market price to reflect the externalities.

This could involve a congestion charge, which makes motorists pay the true social cost of driving into a city centre. For example, the petrol for the journey may cost £3, but the external cost of driving into London is considered to be £15, so the congestion charge is set at £15. This means that the driver ends up paying a total of £18 – the private cost + external cost. The revenue from charging the external cost could then be used to provide improved public transport or free bike hire, both of which are forms of transport with positive externalities. Reducing the cost of other forms of transport relative to driving helps shift transport patterns to a better outcome, which avoids the worst levels of congestion (and pollution).

OVERCOMING EXTERNALITIES

Taxing externalities is known as 'internalizing the externality'. This is because the price we pay after the tax more accurately reflects the full social cost, rather than just the private cost. It is also sometimes referred to as a Pigovian tax after the economist Arthur C. Pigou, who developed the concept of externalities in his book *The Economics of Welfare* (1920). Pigou used the example of drinking alcohol. He argued that excess drinking of alcohol led to many external costs for society – increase in hospital treatments, increased crime and disorder, and higher police costs. Therefore, there is a strong economic case for taxing goods like alcohol and cigarettes. By happy coincidence (from a government's perspective), these taxes become important sources of revenue as demand tends to be price inelastic – increasing price only leads to a small fall in demand (see Elasticity, pages 62–7).

Arthur Pigou.

Taxing alcoholic drinks can help account for their negative externalities.

However, taxation and subsidies are not the only way to deal with the presence of externalities. For example, the government could use behavioural economics to discourage use. Banning advertising and hiding cigarettes from view is an attempt to reduce demand through making it less easy to buy. Similarly, the government could insist that warning labels are placed on 'unhealthy foods' to discourage impulse buys.

Also, it is not always the case that individuals will ignore externalities. For example, a firm may decide to choose more environmentally friendly methods of production either through altruism or a desire to cultivate a better brand image. For example, cosmetic firms who stopped testing on animals saw an improvement in brand image.

DIFFICULTY IN MEASURING EXTERNALITIES

Some decisions on externalities are relatively easy to measure. For example, in terms of traffic congestion, we can attempt to measure the costs of average waiting times and put a value on time. However, other externalities are much harder to measure. For example, what is the externality of building a nuclear power station? Supporters may argue that it has positive externalities because it reduces carbon emissions and provides energy security. However, on the other hand, there is the risk

Decontamination activities after the Chernobyl disaster.

of catastrophic external costs from a nuclear disaster like Chernobyl or Fukushima. In the presence of uncertainty, it is harder to put an external cost value on the decision because we will only know at a later date. For other goods like heroin or cocaine, trying to internalize the externality through taxation would be inappropriate because the damage to the individual could be so great that a complete ban is more appropriate than tax.

Nevertheless, externalities are very important because they are a significant limit on purely free markets. A free market will, by definition, enable individuals and firms to ignore the presence of externalities, which could be very damaging for social welfare. The more externalities there are in production and consumption, the greater the need for either government intervention or self-regulation to improve welfare.

44
Carbon Pricing

Carbon pricing is a policy to tackle environmental pollution by making the producer and consumer pay for the external cost of carbon emissions.

The principle behind carbon pricing is the idea that 'the polluter should pay'. (This is a principle enshrined into international law at the 1992 Rio Environment summit.)

In a free market, burning coal to develop power generates negative externalities, such as CO_2 emissions that contribute to global warming. These negative externalities are borne by the whole world and future generations who will face lower living standards because of our decision to burn coal. The problem is that all these external costs are not borne by the firm and consumer. Therefore the market price of coal is much cheaper than the actual social cost.

A coal power plant.

SOCIAL COST

This is where carbon pricing comes in. If we can place an economic cost on carbon emissions, then the logic is to place a tax on coal – equivalent to this external cost. Suppose coal-powered electricity costs £10 per kilowatt-hour (kwH), but we estimate the negative effect of CO_2 pollution is £5 per kwH. The tax will increase the price of coal-powered electricity by 50% to £15. Consumers will now pay the full social cost. The social cost includes both the private monetary cost, but also those hidden effects to other people (and the environment). In economics, we say the externality has been internalized because the price we pay now includes all the different costs of carbon.

Carbon tax

The aim is to increase the tax so consumers pay for the social marginal cost (SMC).

The advantage is that now we are paying the social price of coal, so there is a strong incentive to reduce consumption. Since coal is more expensive, energy firms will have an incentive to switch to renewable energy, such as that provided by wind power or solar panels. Consumers will have an incentive to try to reduce electricity use, and may

consider installing solar panels. In the short term, demand may be quite inelastic (creating only a small fall in demand). Even when the price of petrol rises, we pay because we need it. However, the longer

Installing solar panels.

the tax remains, the more it creates incentives for firms and consumers to change their behaviour. We won't immediately respond to a higher price, but the next time we buy a car, we may wish to buy electric rather than a petrol-powered car. Also, over time, higher energy prices may encourage households to spend on insulating their homes or installing solar panels.

The downside is that this tax may be a shock to the coal industry. With a fall in demand, firms may make workers redundant because demand falls. However, although this carbon pricing may cause some temporary structural unemployment while coal is phased out, new jobs will be created in alternative energy sources, such as renewable energy.

REVENUE NEUTRAL

Carbon pricing can be politically unpopular because consumers are faced with higher prices and firms with lower profits. However, carbon pricing is designed not to increase the overall tax burden, but to shift taxes onto the areas of production and consumption that cause pollution. For example, suppose the government raised £2 billion from a new carbon tax. It could use all this tax to cut VAT by £2 billion. Therefore, the consumer pays the same level of tax overall, but now it just comes from a different source. In Canada, the government introduced a form of carbon pricing (named pollution pricing), which led to higher energy bills, but the government returned 90% of this new tax back to households in the form of tax rebates. Therefore, households had more or less the same disposable income overall. But they had a stronger incentive to reduce electricity use. Households who were willing to turn down the heating to reduce electricity could avoid some of the tax but still receive the tax rebates and theoretically be better off. The political success of a carbon tax may depend on making the redistribution of the proceeds of a CO_2 tax both effective and visible.

The advantage of a carbon tax is that we don't legislate what people can and cannot consume. If a family really wants to fly around the world, they can, but with a carbon tax, the price is higher. So a carbon tax on flights creates an incentive to take holidays closer to home. This does require the government intervention of setting a tax, but this still appeals to market-oriented economists who argue that the decision on how much to produce and consume is essentially left to the market. It is simpler than a more interventionist approach of stipulating what firms should produce and how.

PROBLEMS OF CARBON TAXES

One criticism of a carbon tax is that it will have more effect on households with low income. For example, higher heating costs could make it hard for the poor and elderly to heat their homes, while the wealthy would be unaffected and just pay the higher prices. However, inequality should not be a reason to stop carbon pricing. If necessary, the proceeds of carbon pricing can be used to reduce inequality by reducing the tax burden on low-income groups. The main thing is that everyone benefits from the reduction in carbon emissions and a better environment.

A bigger concern is that a national carbon tax may shift production to countries without a carbon tax, so that in effect the world starts exporting pollution to countries who most need the investment. For example, if Australia placed a tax on mineral mining because of the carbon emissions, this may create a competitive advantage for countries without a carbon levy and production may just shift to countries without any legislation. However, most carbon taxes can be levelled on consumption, which negates the problem by taxing the end user, rather than the producer.

Another potential problem of carbon taxes is that they can be difficult to administer and regulate. Firstly, it is difficult to know the true external cost of CO_2 emissions – depending on which issues are taken into consideration. More problematic is keeping track of emissions, with a high carbon tax creating an incentive for firms and consumers to avoid

A carbon tax on airline flights would be difficult to avoid, but this would not be the case for all industries.

paying the tax by polluting in secret. Some taxes, like a tax on airline flights, are very hard to avoid, but other carbon taxes could give room for firms to hide emissions, such as the European car industry massaging statistics on fuel emissions.

A final word on carbon taxes is that for some environmental campaigners they don't go far enough. If global warming presents an existential threat to future life on Earth, we shouldn't rely on a market-based approach that allows continued carbon emissions, but instead move immediately to close down coal-powered stations and mandate only renewable energy. A supporter of carbon taxes may counter that this is unnecessary because the only thing that really matters is setting the right level of carbon tax. Set it sufficiently high, and the coal industry will be forced to close down anyway.

45

Oil and Alternative Energy

Oil is the world's most traded commodity for good reason. It is a vital component of any modern economy.

Oil and its derivatives form the basis of modern transport and have many other uses, from plastics to heating and producing electricity.

DRAWBACKS OF OIL

Our dependence on oil has quite a few drawbacks. Firstly, the price is volatile because changes in market demand can lead to big fluctuations in price. The supply of oil, however, is inelastic, at least in the short term. When oil prices rise, producers cannot (or do not necessarily want to) respond by increasing supply quickly. It takes time to dig new oil wells, bring supply on to the market and refine the crude oil into useable products. This leads to surges in the price, which can leave consumers paying much higher prices at the petrol pumps.

A bigger issue with oil is the negative externalities of its consumption. Using oil causes pollution: petrol and diesel fumes are one of the leading

Oil producers may not be able or willing to quickly increase supply in response to price rises.

causes of airborne pollution in major cities, leading to a variety of health problems such as asthma and lung disease. This is a localized cost of using oil, but the bigger issue is the impact of CO_2 emissions on contributing to global warming, which is already causing numerous economic and social problems around the world. The problem is that market forces which determine supply and demand of oil are not taking into account these external costs and so there is a socially inefficient outcome, where the market continues to consume oil despite the costs to the planet.

Another issue regarding oil is that production is dominated by a small number of countries in OPEC. This gives producers a degree of economic and political leverage, which became apparent during the war in Ukraine. Oil importers can face economic and political difficulties during periods of rising prices. For example, after the oil price spike in 2022, Sri Lanka was left unable to import oil, causing major economic disruption.

ALTERNATIVES TO OIL

Since the first Oil Shock in the 1970s, there have been a growing range of alternatives to oil, such as electric and battery-powered energy. With higher oil prices, it is more attractive for producers to invest in developing alternatives. Also, the higher prices of oil have encouraged greater energy efficiency. In the 1960s, US cars were notoriously uneconomical – petrol was so cheap it didn't really matter how fuel-efficient a car was. But, as oil supply was restricted and prices rose, consumers wanted to buy more energy-efficient cars. The result is that in 2022 oil accounts for a smaller share of the economy than it did in the 1970s. It is still the biggest traded commodity, but a rising price has less effect than previously.

THE FALLING PRICE OF RENEWABLES

An interesting phenomenon to note is that as demand for renewable energy has increased, the efficiency of renewable energy has increased beyond many people's expectations. Between 2009 and 2019, the average global price of electricity generated by solar power fell from $359 per megawatt-hour (MWh) to $40 per MWh.

How did the price of solar energy fall so fast? This is a combination of quite a few economic concepts. The first is economies of scale. When output is low, average costs tend to be high, but as production is scaled up, it becomes more efficient to mass produce panels in bigger factories, and so average costs fall. The second concept is called learning curves. As

A solar farm.

firms produce more solar panels, they learn from previous experience and find ways to cut costs, develop new techniques and become more efficient. This causes lower prices and output to expand. Then as output continues to increase, it enables companies to continue to learn more efficient methods of production, and these small incremental gains continue to add up. In the initial phase, solar energy did receive government subsidies. Indeed, one of its very early uses was for satellites in space. In the 1960s, solar energy would have been uneconomical for any ordinary uses. But government support for this niche use enabled solar to get a foothold. Now, there is no need for government subsidies to produce solar panels, as market forces are helping to drop the price of producing electricity from solar panels.

WHY IT IS HARD TO SWITCH

In 2020, the price of generating electricity from wind power and solar panels is cheaper than from old fossil fuels like coal and oil. So why are we still dependent on oil and fossil fuels? The reason is that the cost of producing electricity is not the only factor, but whether the infrastructure can support a shift away from oil. Electric cars are cheaper to run than petrol cars, but to buy a new electric car is a significant investment, which only the high-income households could consider. For many modes of transport, trucks, aeroplanes and ships, the raw power needed means that battery-operated electric power is not realistic at the present time. Another factor behind the difficulty of switching to alternative energy

A Tesla electric car.

sources is the pressure on land. Energy from inland wind power is one of the cheapest sources of energy. Yet, it requires substantial amounts of land that people in densely populated countries may not be willing to accept. The same is true for solar energy.

However, given the environmental benefits of reducing oil consumption, there is a hope that market forces and technological improvements will continue to make renewable energy more practical in a greater range of uses. Given the past trends in improved renewable energy, we are likely to see renewables have an increasingly large competitive edge. However, those concerned about the environment say waiting on market forces is not enough. We need a plan to accelerate the shift by discouraging fossil fuels and subsidizing the use of renewables.

46
The Sunk Cost Fallacy

The sunk cost fallacy is the observation that humans can make the mistake of continuing with a project because of the past investment they have already made, ignoring the fact that a more rational approach would be to forget past investments and cancel the project.

IRRETRIEVABLE COSTS

A sunk cost is an irretrievable cost. It is an investment we have made and cannot get back. For example, if a firm spent £100 million investing in a new personal calculator, this research and development is sunk; the firm can't ask for it back because once wages have been paid, the money is gone. However, after a few years of inventing this new personal calculator, the firm may realize it made a mistake: the market for personal calculators is falling because consumers are now making use of their smartphones rather than buying a separate calculator. But if a firm is 50% of its way through the project, what does it do? Spend another £100 million to bring the calculator to market? It may estimate that the revenue on sales will amount to only £70 million – giving a net loss of £30 million to continue from this point.

Therefore, a rational firm may decide to end the project immediately and write off that £100 million of past investment. However, in the real

If a firm spends a significant sum investing in a calculator, they may realize the release of the smartphone removes the need for their product – the investment is a sunk cost.

Concorde is one of the most famous examples of the sunk cost fallacy.

world, the managers who authorized the project may be horrified at the prospect of writing off £100 million of investment with nothing to show for it. So they continue the project – even though doing so will lead to a bigger loss. This is the sunk cost fallacy, the past investment influencing a current decision. Stop now, and lose £100 million. Continue, and lose £100 million + the £30 million net loss from poor sales, giving a net loss of £130 million. But what looms large in the mind of the business executives is having to write off an investment of £100 million and acknowledge making a poor decision.

CONCORDE

Another good example of the sunk cost fallacy is the development of Concorde. In 1962, the initial cost to develop the plane was £70 million. By 1976, the cost had increased to £1.5 billion. Not only that, but oil prices were now much higher, making Concorde even less attractive as it was very fuel-inefficient. Also, the sonic boom in flight and concerns over safety caused potential buyers to drop out. Concorde would never be profitable and would have to be run at a loss, with the development costs being absorbed by the British and French governments. As the costs mounted and market conditions changed, it would have been rational to stop the loss-making project before more losses were incurred. But, because so much investment had been poured in and it had become symbolic of British and French cooperation, the governments were unwilling to pull the plug and the plane continued to be developed and built. The initial investment costs were never recouped before the plane was dropped from active service in 2003.

PERSONAL SUNK COSTS

On a personal level, the issue of sunk costs can occur in a variety of ways. Suppose you buy a monthly membership to a gym. But after one

Annual gym membership becomes a sunk cost once paid.

month you feel under the weather. If you had not paid any membership, you wouldn't even consider paying to go to the gym. But, because your membership has already been paid, you feel like you should go – to get your money's worth. You have paid £40, and if you don't go, it is wasted. However, to maximize your utility, you should really be asking yourself: will I get satisfaction from going to the gym or not? If you feel ill and going to the gym makes it worse, you should forget the fact you paid £40 and recognize that going to the gym will make you feel more ill.

Suppose you bought a flat in the city centre for £100,000, but now have the chance to move to a more desirable place in the suburbs for a house costing £150,000. You just about have the funds to buy the £150,000 house, but the problem is that house prices in the city centre have fallen post-COVID. Someone offers you £93,000, but you are unwilling to sell for a loss. You feel you should wait until your initial purchase price of £100,000 is met. However, if you wait to regain your sunk cost of the £100,000 purchase price, the opportunity to move may fall through. This is why when deciding whether to sell or not, the price we paid at the start shouldn't be a dominant factor. The key issue is: what is a good price now? If you bought shares and they fell 10%, it may be better to sell and accept a 10% loss, rather than risk an even bigger loss in the future.

IS THE SUNK COST FALLACY REALLY A FALLACY?

Economics textbooks assume that the overriding goal is to maximize profit and financial returns. In this case, there is often a sunk cost fallacy because managers make bigger losses rather than stop investment projects halfway through. However, in the real world, profit maximization is not the only goal that people consider important. From the perspective of the firm that developed a personal calculator, stopping halfway through a big project might lead to reputational damage. People may pour scorn on a firm who invested so much and then gave up. If the firm keeps going, the benefit to its reputation may make the financial loss worthwhile.

Suppose a firm invests millions in advertising a new brand. This advertising is a sunk cost. If the brand was an initial failure and the firm decided to drop it straight away, this wouldn't look good to consumers. Sometimes it is important to keep up appearances even if there is a net financial loss. The same was true for Concorde. Developing such a prestigious super-speed aircraft reflected well on British and French technological capacity. Decades later, Concorde is still the world's most recognizable aeroplane and excites people's imagination. These are benefits that cannot be easily included in a profit and loss balance sheet.

Finally, what about personal choices like going to the gym? Why do we agree to sign up to a monthly gym membership or pay for several lessons in advance for learning a foreign language? The answer is that if we pay for a whole year in advance, we are motivated to go to the gym when we don't feel like it. In other words, we want the sunk cost of our annual gym membership to weigh over us. If we had to pay every time we went to the gym, that would be a reason not to go. But payment in advance is motivation to try and get our money's worth.

So, we should be willing to ignore sunk costs when they don't favour us, but equally we should recognize that profit and loss is not the only factor we should take into account.

Sunk costs may drag down a business, but if you look beyond the profit motive, there may be occasions when the greater financial loss is acceptable because of the other benefits the investment provides.

47

Luddite Fallacy

When a worker loses a job because of the deployment of new technology, there is an understandable tendency to believe it is the technology that is causing unemployment.

But this belief that new technology causes overall unemployment to rise is a mistake and caused by looking at only part of the overall situation.

HOW NEW TECHNOLOGY CREATES JOBS

When new technology is introduced into an economy, some workers do indeed lose their jobs. If a supermarket takes delivery of self-service checkouts and staff at manual tills are made redundant, they may, understandably, blame the new self-service machines for taking their jobs. However, this new technology is creating many other effects in the economy. Firstly, there are jobs created in developing and making the technology itself. Therefore, there may be fewer jobs in supermarkets, but there will be more jobs in IT and software development. But there is also another hidden effect behind the new technology. With the new technology, the supermarket can employ fewer workers, and therefore average costs will be lower and firms can cut prices. If the average householder pays lower prices for their weekly shopping, then, almost unnoticed, they will have more disposable income left over. With this higher disposable income, they will be able to spend more on going out, leisure and entertainment.

The knock-on effect is that new jobs will be created in these new sectors. The supermarket staff who may lose their jobs from self-service machines may soon be able to find new jobs in other sectors.

Self-service checkout machines.

THE PAST 200 YEARS AND UNEMPLOYMENT

Another way to think about the Luddite fallacy is to consider all the technological advances of the past 200 years and ask what has happened to unemployment in this period. Allowing for cyclical fluctuations, general unemployment has remained very similar. Of course, the nature of the economy has changed dramatically. Two hundred years ago, 90% of the working population was employed in agriculture, but modern farm machinery made this labour redundant. As they lost jobs on the farm, workers moved to the factories and towns. But continued technological progress caused most of these jobs to be replaced eventually by machines and higher productivity. All the time, technology increased the efficiency of production and average incomes in society grew, enabling us to devote more money to a wider variety of goods and services, causing income to permanently increase and new jobs to be created.

The Luddite fallacy is so called after a group of nineteenth-century textile workers who felt threatened by new spinning machines which replaced the traditional artisan approach to making clothes. It is true that these individual workers lost out, but if we had stayed at the levels of technology available in 1800, our choice of clothes and our living standards would now be significantly lower. In the past 100 years, there are numerous examples of whole industries wiped out by new technology, causing the loss of numerous jobs – but any unemployment created by these changes was just temporary.

Luddites smashing new machines.

THIS TIME IS DIFFERENT

The interesting thing about the Luddite fallacy is that no matter how frequently overall unemployment is unaffected by new technology, we still retain the fear that this time things will be different. For example, it is feared that artificial intelligence and powerful robots will be able to replace the labour of skilled workers, such as drivers, nurses, doctors and accountants – all workers previously immune from technology. In effect, there will be no job safe from the march of technology. But, even if this were to happen, the same logic should apply. With robots we could

Is this the future?
A robot surgeon.

save countless amounts of money, if we don't need to pay doctors and accountants; the price of many goods would continue to fall and we would enjoy better living standards and pay for new services or just enjoy more leisure time. This fall in costs and more disposable income would enable new, unexpected industries. Some people with high income would prefer to pay for a human teacher / doctor than a soulless robot. The point is that new technology and improved productivity gives the economy more income and a better range of options. It could even involve paying a universal basic income to make sure everyone benefits from the new technology.

STRUCTURAL UNEMPLOYMENT

Over time, it is true that new technology does create new job opportunities elsewhere in the economy. But, for the short term, some workers can face very real economic hardship. If a steel worker loses their job due to new technology, he may be unable to gain a new job in IT or leisure services because he lacks the necessary skills. New technology may devastate a certain region. For example, if technology impacts the mining industries, regions with a high concentration of miners may see very high levels of unemployment because it is difficult to move to other areas of the economy. Therefore, there is a very real cost from introducing new technology. Therefore, although new technology should benefit society in the long term, a period of rapid transition may create a very real unemployment issue in regions left behind from this move to better technology.

COULD THE LUDDITE FALLACY BE TRUE?

While there are good reasons to dismiss many fears about new technology, there is a scenario where the Luddite fallacy is indeed true, and new technology does cause a significant number of people to be unemployed. Suppose the major new technological advances are made by a few large multinational companies with very significant market power, such as Amazon, Apple, Google and Tesla. These companies then replace workers with new technology and increase the efficiency of production. However, their monopoly power means that they do not pass the efficiency savings onto consumers in the form of lower prices but instead take advantage to increase prices. In this scenario, the benefits of technology are captured by the company, which makes higher profits, and not the average householder, who enjoys lower prices. Therefore, although there is more income in society, some households are not seeing it. In fact, they may have lost good jobs to artificial intelligence and also be facing rising prices. If the government collected more corporation tax, they could give benefits to the unemployed. But, if the companies keep profit in tax havens, society is unable to access this increase in wealth. Therefore, where a few monopolies dominate and many workers do not find a good replacement job, it is possible that overall unemployment may rise.

The number of miners has fallen in recent years.

48
Creative Destruction

Creative destruction is a term used to describe how capitalism is constantly changing and evolving.

Part of this change and growth involves allowing inefficient firms to go out of business. Even if this results in temporary unemployment and the loss of output, it is necessary in the long term to allow for new ideas, new products and new firms to come to the fore.

The term creative destruction was coined by the economist Joseph Schumpeter. Schumpeter was taken by the ideas of Karl Marx, who wrote about capitalism's tendency to break things through wars and economic crisis. Marx saw this periodic crisis of capitalism as wasting resources and causing damage to workers. However, Schumpeter saw this in a very different light. It is only through constant change, he argued, that an economy can grow and create the incentive for higher productivity and new ideas and technology to be born.

Joseph Schumpeter.

> *The fundamental impulse that sets and keeps the capitalist engine in motion comes from the new consumers' goods, the new methods of production or transportation, the new markets, the new forms of industrial organization that capitalist enterprise creates.*

Joseph Schumpeter, Capitalism, Socialism and Democracy (1942)

There is considerable overlap here with the Luddite fallacy because it stems from the observation that when bad things seem to happen – workers

A closed shop on a high street. Will a better firm take its place?

lose jobs because of new technology – there are good things happening to the economy elsewhere. One great limitation of the Soviet command economy was that many state-owned industries were not allowed to fail. No worker was supposed to be made redundant. Therefore, no matter how inefficient and unproductive a state-owned industry was, it was guaranteed not to fail. The problem is this created a perverse incentive. Rather than try to introduce new ideas and working practices, it became easier to stay static. Therefore, firms which would have gone out of business in capitalist economies were supported in the Soviet system.

THE IMPORTANCE OF NEW INNOVATION

Creative destruction is important because it supports a laissez-faire, or free market-style, approach to the economy. The threat of getting left behind by the competition causes firms to seek to continually improve their business, reducing costs and developing new products. If a firm does become unprofitable, it is a sign that they were using resources inefficiently. By going out of business, workers and resources can move to something more productive. For example, suppose that in the inner city, there was a large record shop, which was seeing a big drop in sales due to digital downloads. The shop may employ 100 people and occupy prime retail space. If it closes down, its retail space is boarded up and 100 people lose their jobs. But the space is then free for a new firm to start up. A new firm may use the space to create a mix of office and work spaces for digital content creators, which are in high demand. The closure of the shop has allowed a new firm with higher productivity to take its place. The threat of closure may also be a spur for a business to change its way of operating. For example, if a newspaper saw the

A closed coal breaker in the Rust Belt of the US, Ashley, Pennsylvania.

sales of hard copy papers fall, it may invest in an online news site with paywall to collect a new form of revenue. Without the switch to online and a paywall, it might go out of business.

If we look back at the past 100 years, the top companies have been constantly changing. The 50 largest companies in the post-war period look very different today. Many traditional retailers have been forced out of business because they have been outmanoeuvred by new competitors such as Walmart and Amazon, who have found new ways of cutting costs and bringing an innovative approach to business. On the negative side, we have lost many traditional retailers such as Woolworths; on the positive side, we have seen lower prices for many staple goods.

COSTS OF CREATIVE DESTRUCTION

From an academic standpoint, it is easy to write about the virtues of creative destruction and laissez-faire economics. In the long term, the destruction and reinvention of business has caused rising living standards and a greater choice of goods. But this is not to say there are not real-life costs affected by this process of creative destruction. When inefficient firms are left to go out of business, some workers may experience several years of structural unemployment as they struggle to find new employment. Also, when an industry closes down, it may not necessarily be replaced. The Rust Belt refers to states in the Midwest and Northeastern America which saw a decline in manufacturing, but where new jobs and enterprise did not spring up to replace these industries. In fact, regional decline set in, encouraging people to migrate away, causing inner cities to become neglected and bringing a corresponding rise in social problems. New industries were being created but mainly in big cities, which led to overpopulation and a shortage of housing.

Market forces only consider profit and not wider issues such as social welfare. For example, in the 1920s, the US automobile industry grew rapidly, and with the help of car-friendly legislation it was able to put out of business train and bus companies, making city centres dedicated to automobiles. In one sense, this was progress: the car was a great invention that increased freedom and reduced the cost of transport, but there have also been costs. Cars create negative externalities of pollution, congestion and traffic accidents. US cities are dominated by cars, and this makes them a less attractive place to live. When local public transport is forced out of business, we can say this is creative destruction, but we also lose the social benefits of a public transport system.

A final point is that in a severe recession, good and efficient firms may be pushed out of business – just because of current market conditions. For example, in the 2009 recession, the US automobile industry was close to bankruptcy. Some argued that it was best to leave things to the market – if the big firms went bust, this would be best in the long term – but the government decided to intervene and bail out the car firms. As the economy recovered, so did the car industry, turning itself around. If the process of creative destruction had been allowed to take its course, this reversal could not have happened.

Creative destruction ignores the role of externalities in a laissez-faire economy. The rise of cars and consequent fall of public transport has led to increased pollution and traffic in several US cities.

49
Impact of Immigration

Immigration is often a contentious political issue because of the cultural, social and economic implications related to a large influx of people from abroad.

If an economy experiences large net migration, there are differing opinions about whether there is an economic benefit or not. One concern about immigration is that an increase in the supply of labour will push down wages and make it harder for native-born workers to retain employment. The argument is based on a simple supply and demand analysis: if supply increases, wage rates fall.

DOES IT REDUCE WAGES?

However, this looks at the labour market in isolation because net migration does not affect just the supply of labour but the demand too. If there are more people living, working and spending in an economy, overall demand for goods and services will rise, and hence there will be an increase in

Immigration and wages

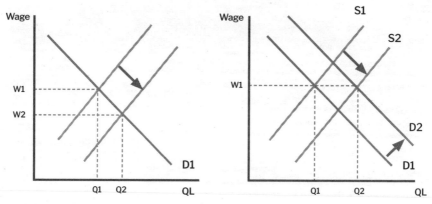

An increase in the supply of labour causes lower wages. But, if demand increases too, then wages stay the same.

Immigration to New York City, 1887.

demand for labour equivalent to the increase in supply. Net migration is essentially similar to a rise in the population: there are more people and therefore the overall size of the economy grows. Therefore, on its own net migration is unlikely to affect overall wage rates too much.

However, if net migration is focused on low-skilled workers without qualifications, the labour market will see a disproportionate rise in unskilled labour willing to work for lower wages. In this case, unskilled native workers could see a fall in sector wages because the increased competition for their jobs is not met by a corresponding rise in demand. Skilled workers will be unaffected by this kind of migration.

There have been innumerable studies on the impact of migration and the picture is often mixed. Migration can lead to lower wages for unskilled workers, but the effect is often quite limited.

EFFECT ON UNEMPLOYMENT

A big fear of immigration is that it will cause unemployment. If net migration occurs in a period of high unemployment, it may appear that the extra labour force is magnifying the problem of unemployment because the recession means that there isn't sufficient demand in the economy. However, again the problem there is not the migration but the state of the economy. An economy in recession will not be able to absorb the extra labour force

Reasons for migration

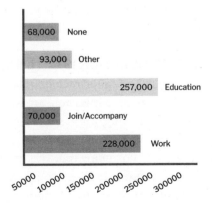

68,000	None
93,000	Other
257,000	Education
70,000	Join/Accompany
228,000	Work

50000   100000   150000   200000   250000   300000

because there is already a job shortage. However, when the economy recovers, the greater number of people will find work because there is the dual effect of higher labour supply and higher labour demand.

In practical terms, during periods of high unemployment and recession, the motivation for net migration falls considerably, so there is a self-regulating fall in migration when jobs are not available. Ireland had a large influx of construction workers during the boom years of the early 2000s, but when the housing market turned and house prices started to fall, the migration rate fell dramatically. The unemployment rate stabilized as the economic situation caused many to return to their native country rather than stay unemployed in Ireland. Also, if we look at economies with very high rates of net migration, such as the United States around the turn of the 19th/20th century, it was quite compatible with high job creation.

AGE PROFILE OF MIGRANTS

Another factor that determines the effectiveness of net migration is the age profile of workers. If migrants are young and of working age, this can boost the economy in terms of increasing the labour force and reducing the dependency ratio. People of working age are net contributors to the government budget because they pay the most income tax but do not receive the biggest government benefits of pensions. Also, healthcare spending goes disproportionately to older people. Therefore, net migration can improve public finances because the new workers are net contributors. This point may become increasingly salient as many Western economies are facing very low birth rates and a rapidly ageing population. This ageing population is putting pressure on government finances because of higher pension and healthcare spending. Young working age migrants can help improve the government's fiscal position and also help to fill in the many job vacancies, such as care workers and healthcare staff.

WHY IMMIGRATION IS OFTEN UNPOPULAR

Often migrants are attracted to move to a country because of the economic opportunities, so migrants are more likely to be of working age. Hence, in theory, net migration should give overall economic benefits of higher GDP and improved public finances, and help to fill unpopular job vacancies. For example, free movement of people in the European Union has led to quite strong flows of working people from east to west. This has led to some economic benefits, but has often been unpopular,

Brussels – the densely populated capital of Belgium, where a large population helps create economies of scale.

and it was a factor in the UK's decision to leave the European Union. Why are the economic benefits not visible? Firstly, migration is usually concentrated in particular areas, so there tends to be a visible increase in the population in certain areas. This places greater pressure on road congestion, housing, public services and amenities. From a macroeconomic perspective, public finances may well be improved, but people living in certain areas may not see any visible investment, just longer waiting lists and more expensive accommodation. In theory, the government could use improved tax revenues to invest in housing and public services, but they may be dealing with their own financial constraints and not do so, meaning that local people just see the downside of more people in an area.

We tend to assume that increased population density has a negative effect, and there can indeed be real issues. When supply is limited, the price of renting property rises faster than inflation and wages. But higher population density can also have advantages. There are economies of scale from greater population density, with mass transit and public investment giving a better rate of return with higher density. It is also good for the environment in the sense that the net carbon emission per person is considerably lower in densely populated areas like a city compared to rural areas. Countries such as Belgium and the Netherlands with high population density can have good standards of living as the economy adjusts to this density.

50
Housing Market

Like many other markets, the housing market is influenced by supply and demand, but the housing market has particular importance for households and the wider economy.

In recent years, many housing markets in Asia, Europe and America have witnessed above-inflation house price increases, causing buying a house or renting property to become very expensive. For people in urban areas, up to 50% of their disposable income can go on rent or a mortgage, making housing a big drag on living standards. Why did house prices become so expensive and who are the winners and losers? In the United Kingdom house prices have risen faster than inflation and faster than earnings. In the mid-1990s, average house prices were just under three times average earnings. By 2022, that ratio had reached seven times average earnings.

The ratio of house prices to earnings has increased.

To understand this increase in house prices, we can make use of simple supply and demand analysis. In densely populated regions, building new houses is challenging. We tend to value the diminishing areas of green space and so resist the idea of building new houses. In big cities, there is very little available space for building the quantity of housing needed to meet increased demand. This limit of supply is crucial for pushing up house prices faster than inflation. However, it is not the only factor to consider.

Demand has been rising for several reasons. Firstly, even countries with limited population growth can see a faster rise in the number of households. We no longer live in extended families, and increasingly people live alone. The result is a rise in the number of households, which is greater than the population. Also, between 2008 and 2022 we saw another phenomenon that made buying houses increasingly attractive. To combat low economic growth, central banks cut interest rates to very low levels. This made it attractive to buy a house through mortgage borrowing. With interest rates close to zero, saving money in a bank or buying bonds offered poor returns. As an alternative, investors could buy a house through borrowing at low cost and then benefit from decent rentable income and capital gains through rising house prices. Therefore, rising prices changed the composition of home buys; rather than buying to live, investors have increasingly been buying to let. The strong growth of house prices has only made it more attractive to try and get on the property bandwagon.

Effects on house prices

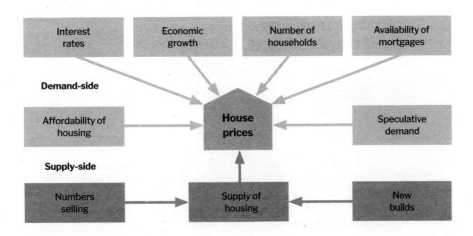

217

WHO BENEFITS, AND WHO LOSES?

The problem with high house prices is that it creates winners and losers. The winners are the landlords and buy-to-let investors who have benefited from capital appreciation and good income flows. The strong returns from housing creates a virtuous cycle, at least for them: they can reinvest profit into buying more houses, thus pushing up prices still further. The losers are young people who find buying a house to be out of their reach and therefore have to use the rentable property market, where rents have also outstripped inflation, due to shortage of housing. Renting requires a large monthly outlay, but there is no investment or option to pay off a mortgage for retirement. The 'generation rent' who are unable to buy will find their retirement very different when they have to keep paying rent even after they have retired and are no longer earning.

HOUSE PRICE CRASHES

Of course, it is easy to fall into the trap of thinking that supply and demand factors will always keep pushing house prices higher. There are certainly reasons to believe that house prices will always remain relatively expensive, but this doesn't mean they can't fall, such as in the property crash of 2006–2008. In the summer of 2022, central banks started to raise interest rates in response to high inflation. The problem is that as interest rates start to rise, the motivation for buying a house suddenly changes as investors see their returns falling. Combined with lower economic growth and falling real incomes, these factors can suddenly cause a shift in consumer confidence and investors may start to sell their properties before prices fall further. In the United States and countries like Spain and Ireland, house prices fell up to 50% in response to the credit crunch of the Global Financial Crisis as market conditions

Increasing house prices make it difficult for young people to buy their first property.

radically changed. The fall in UK prices was more muted at 20%, but only due to a greater shortage of supply. So if an estate agent or mortgage salesman ever tries to tell you that this time is different and house prices will never fall, be very careful.

THE IMPORTANCE OF THE HOUSING MARKET

The housing market itself can have an influence on the wider economy. It is the biggest form of personal wealth, with between 50% and 70% of households being owner-occupied (depending on the country). If house prices rise, this creates a positive wealth effect. Those who own a house feel more confident because their main asset increases in value. Also, with higher house prices, they can remortgage their house to gain equity to spend on other items. In the UK, where property ownership has reached 70%, a booming housing market can have a positive influence on consumer spending. In the late 1980s, rising house prices helped fuel an economic boom. But, when house prices fall, consumer confidence evaporates as assets fall. A large fall in house prices can also cause bank losses because if they repossess homes which failed to meet mortgage payments, they will gain less than the value of the mortgage. This was a big problem in 2008, when banks had to write off billions from failed mortgages and as a result reduced their lending. In countries with lower property ownership rates, falling house prices may have less impact because some young people may benefit from cheaper rents and cheaper property prices. But the overriding issue is usually the loss of consumer confidence from falling prices.

When house prices rise, so does consumer spending, but when they fall consumer confidence falls as well.

INDEX

Picture Credits

t = top, b = bottom

Alamy: 69, 83, 87, 100, 113, 116, 144, 165b, 184, 188t, 208

Flickr: 189

Getty Images: 28, 106, 127, 151

Library of Congress: 98, 112, 213

Shutterstock: 8, 9 (x2), 11, 16, 18, 29, 30, 31, 32, 36, 37, 41, 46, 50, 51, 52, 56, 58 (x2), 59, 61, 63, 64, 66, 68, 72, 75, 85, 96, 102, 108, 110, 122, 133, 146, 148, 149, 150, 154, 159, 161, 165t, 172 (x2), 173, 178, 179, 181, 186, 187, 188b, 191, 192, 194, 196, 198, 199, 200 (x2), 201, 202, 203, 204, 206, 207, 209, 211, 215, 218, 219

Wellcome Collection: 21, 77

Wikimedia Commons: 33, 34, 38, 44, 73, 78, 107, 115, 118, 134, 135, 167, 170, 171, 175, 177, 205, 210